Forward

First published in 1977, ME NO ME was created as a monthly magazine that covered a wide variety of topics on the antique arts in Japan. Now in its 43rd year of publication, the magazine has been read and supported by art collectors and enthusiasts, as well as antique art dealers, art galleries and museums.

Although the core content of ME NO ME focuses on Japanese art, the magazine also covers Chinese, Korean and other antiques originating in East Asia, all of which had great influence on Japanese art. Antique arts from the Orient (Central Asia) and Europe are also occasionally featured.

Often referred to as an Island Nation of the Far East, Japan has been the benefactor of outside influences that made its way across the sea from the Eurasian Continent, whether that be philosophy, literature, or artifacts. All that rich culture has nurtured the unique formation of Japan's sense of beauty and art. It is interesting to see that the arts, artifacts and even culture that has been lost at its original birthplace can often be found in Japan today, as if they had been placed in a time capsule.

As well as further developing imported culture, the Island Nation also found value in preserving the art and the skills inherent to the original beauty of its land. These were sometimes strongly influenced from the imported culture, and at other times strongly contradicted them, but as a result, Japanese culture and art developed in a unique and stratified way.

In our effort to introduce the full beauty and appeal of antique art, ME NO ME dedicates each issue to a theme ranging from the earthenware of the Prehistoric Jomon period (10,000 BCE – 300 BCE) to antique arts from Ancient, Medieval, Early Modern and Modern periods. Each issue offers insightful descriptions and stories behind the featured antique art along with colorful pictures to convey their beauty in their entirety.

In publishing this English-language issue for the first time, we selected features from our past library of more than 500 issues, focusing on interviews and stories of art collectors and art dealers that represent the current antique art scene of Japan. We hope that this issue becomes an opportunity for you to discover the fascinating world of Japanese antique art.

ME NO ME

Contents

Cover Design: Yoshikazu Kasai
Photo by Akira Takemae
Details available on page 36-53 in the Breathing Life into an antique feature.

BLUE AND WHITE STEM CUP WITH MYTHICAL
WINGED SEA DRAGON AND WAVE DESIGN
Xuande mark and period, 15th century
Hight 7.6 cm

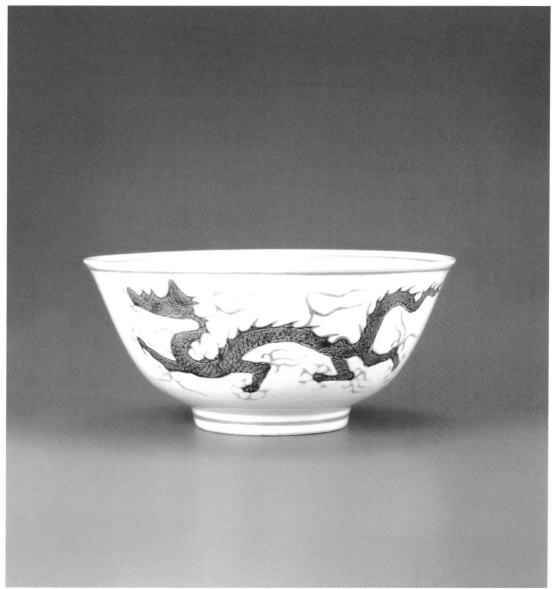

SPECIAL INTERVIEW

SUGIMOTO HIROSHI

A contemporary artist globally active in a wide variety of genres, Sugimoto Hiroshi was scheduled to hold four different exhibitions in Japan in 2020. Unfortunately, the worldwide pandemic has forced some of these events to be postponed. We had the opportunity to sit down and speak to him about the exhibitions and what he thinks the future holds.

Text : Keita Fukazawa

Signs of divine presence behind Japanese Artistry —Sugimoto Hiroshi

– You've been very active, scheduling four exhibitions in 2020 alone. The first one was held at the newly constructed Higashiyama Cube gallery, in part to commemorate the incarnation of the Kyoto City KYOCERA Museum. The exhibition was titled HIROSHI SUGIMOTO – POST VITAM.

Sugimoto: The site of the Kyoto City KYOCERA Museum is actually where Hossho-ji Temple, one of the Rokusho-ji temples (collective name of six Superior Temples), once stood. It was endowed by Emperor Shirakawa in this Okazaki area where he started his *Insei* (cloistered rule) in 11th century. In the years that followed, Taira no Kiyomori founded the Sanjusangen-do, formally known as the Rengeo-in Hondo (Rengeo-in Hall), to appease the vengeful spirit of the late Emperor Sutoku and to ensure a place in the *jodo* (pure land after death) of Buddhism for Emperor Go-Shirakawa. The area has historically been

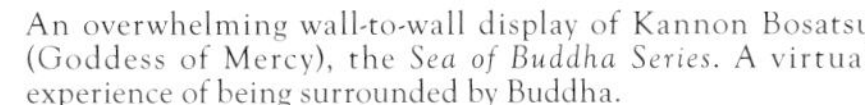

An overwhelming wall-to-wall display of Kannon Bosatsu (Goddess of Mercy), the *Sea of Buddha Series*. A virtual experience of being surrounded by Buddha.

entwined in political and spiritual values. With such history in mind, I wanted to attribute the venue as a temple and design a virtual *jodo* (pure land) to think about the ultimate destiny of death.

Jodo is the center piece of the Japanese people's understanding of death in Buddhism. It is my belief that humans became humans when they were able to embrace the concept of death. Upon the awareness of death, man was able to understand the perception of time. I think this ultimately led to the start of civilization, shaping understandings like planting crops in the spring to harvest in the fall. However, in modern day Japan, the concept of death has lost its original significance. Through my photographic work, I have been exploring the origins of concepts and understandings. This exhibition was my attempt to explore and replicate the *jodo* (pure land), the world after death.

– The exhibition included your photo titled *Sea of Buddha*, as well as the first official showing of the photographs from your OPTICKS series. Antique *ruri* glass (lapis lazuli) items were also on display adjacent to your photographs. In the garden, you had displayed the *Glass Tea House - Mondrian*.

Sugimoto: Taking a photograph means to capture a moment in time. Glass is a substance that has a significant effect in photography and light. When I took the picture of the central image in the temple to create the *Sea of Buddha*, I removed from the surrounding area every item that was placed after the Kamakura period (1185-1333). I wanted to capture the Buddha when the temple was originally founded in the Kamakura period. I had all the lights turned off and took the photograph utilizing the natural rays of light that beamed through the *shoji* (traditional Japanese partitions made from paper).

With OPTICKS, I used sunlight polarized through a prism and took the photos with a polaroid camera...but looking back, I amaze myself for not staying focused on just taking pictures but expanding into spatial design and even getting into things like Noh (traditional Japanese theater) and architecture. Sometimes, I'm not sure what my profession is.

Hyogu Art – The Art of Mounting Art, Sugimoto style

– You had another exhibition occurring at around the same time titled *Frame of Japan*. It was held at the Hosomi Museum where you have been featured twice before.

Sugimoto: Yes, the first exhibition I did was *Art and Leisure – Misenkyo*, which explored food and *tokokazari* (art objects for display in traditional Japanese alcove). The second exhibition, *Mappo* (Apocalypse) featured antique Buddhist art from the Heian period (794-1185), in which I attempted to replicate the sense of beauty possessed by the mysterious collector who went by the pseudonym "Musekian." The most recent exhibition was themed around *hyogu* (art mounting). It has been about twenty years since I started to do my own *hyogu*, but I have only recently been able to establish something that I can call my

Roof Tile from Hosshoji
Heian period
Private Collection.

Model of Go'O shrine
Appropriate Proportion, (2003);
collection of Odawara Art Foundation.

Nanpo Ōta (Shokusanjin)
How to boil *Sōmen* noodle
Late Edo Period (mounted in 2019)
private collection

Kazuo Shiraga
An abstract image with black strokes
Early 1960s (mounted in 2019)
private collection

own, a Sugimoto Style so to speak, such as the ratio of space at the top and bottom of the *hyogu*. I prefer the *hashira* (pillar or space on both sides of the main subject of display) to be as narrow as possible, and I often omit the use of *futai* (a ribbon-like ornament that hangs from the top).

– You have mounted pieces by many famous contemporary artists like Andy Warhol and Kazuo Shiraga.

Sugimoto: Yes, but this piece by Kazuo Shiraga has an interesting story. I found it at an antique flea market in bad condition, with tack marks and folds on the side. It was priced so cheap; I don't think anyone realized its true value. The artist is known for his avant-garde paintings, his use of red paint and drawing with his feet. This piece is his earlier work, but I took the red color image of his later works in selecting the *kogire* (antique cloth) and also colored the *jikusaki* (end of the wooden pole placed at top and bottom) with vermillion lacquer. The exhibition was in part a proposition that *hyogu* (art mounting) itself can be art, as well as introducing the collections of the Hosomi Museum.

Resurrecting the Journey of the Kasuganokami

– In the winter of 2021, you have a plan to hold an exhibition at the Kanagawa Prefectural Kanazawa-Bunko Museum titled *The Journey of the Divine Spirit of Kasuga – From Hitachi to Yamato by Hiroshi Sugimoto*. We understand that this exhibition was to be held in conjunction with the permission granted to the Odawara Art Foundation Enoura Observatory to become a branch shrine of the Kasugataisha (Kasugataisha Shrine).

Sugimoto: When we were constructing the Enoura Observatory, we were blessed to obtain historically significant materials like the cornerstones of the Wakakusagaran excavated from Horyuji (Horyu Temple) and the restored Meigetsu Gate originating from Meigetsu-In (Meigetsu Temple) in Kamakura that was relocated to Nezu Museum. These are items that could not be purchased. The Enoura Observatory, where these precious architectural artifacts were relocated, is like a jodo-styled garden overlooking the Sagami Bay as its "garden pond," but I always felt that it was missing something. Then, in my dreams, I realized it was missing a place to worship the

Hiroshi Sugimoto
Kegon waterfall, 1977 (Mounted in 2005)
collection of Odawara Art Foundation

Jizō Bosatsu (Ksitigarbha)
Kamakura Period (Mounted in 2019)
Private Collection

spirit of the land, a Chinjyu-no-Mori (a forest to worship the Shinto deities).

As to why we had approached Kasugataisha, there is a deep connection there, as if it was something we were destined to follow. The first antique art that I had purchased was the Kasuga shika mandala. After that, items like the Kishimojubosatsu statue and Kasugawakamiya Mandala, which have very strong associations with Kasugataisha, were added to our collection. Therefore, this was something that made us feel that there was a deep connection with Kasuga Shinko (Faith of Kasuga).

– Kasugataisha is famous for being the guardian god of the Fujiwara family, but we were surprised to find out that it had a historical association with Kashima Jingu (Kashima Jingu shrine) of then Hitachi-no-kuni (current region of Ibaraki prefecture).

Sugimoto: Yes, it's known as the Kashima-dachi (Kashima coming). Legend has it, Takemikazuchi no Mikoto (the God of Thunder) descended to Kasuga from Kashima Jingu riding on the back of a white deer. The significance of this story is thought to be that Yamato Chotei (Imperial courts of Yamato) had allowed a regional god to be worshipped after the land had been conquered. Without much thought, we connected Kashima Jingu and Kasugataisha with a straight line on a map, and lo and behold, the location of the Enoura Observatory sat right on the line. Thinking that this was no coincidence, we immediately approached Kasugataisha for its blessing to be enacted as a branch shrine. We have recently intensified our studies on Kasuga Shinko and discovered a new theory in understanding the identity of the Buddhist monk who appears in the Kasugawakamiya Mandala. We have created a graphic diagram about our discovery which was displayed at the exhibition.

Japanese antique art that stands out in the world

– Sugimoto's activities have always explored the roots of Japanese culture and it seems to lead to the question of what defines Japanese as a race.

Sugimoto: Even today, I believe, the Japanese people have a state of mind inherited from the Jomon period (10,000 BCE – 300 BCE). For example, when we placed a stone statue inside a glass shrine located within the *Kaseki-kutsu*

Front : Kasuga Deer Deity
Kamakura Period
(sakaki tree/saddle/antlers: Yoshihiro Suda 2010)
collection of Odawara Art Foundation

Back : Kasuga Wakamiya Mandala
Kamakura Period
collection of Odawara Art Foundation

Odawara Art Foundation / Enoura Observatory

Located on the southside of Odawara City, the Observatory was constructed on a hilltop with a panoramic view of Sagami Bay. The art space offers a gallery space, an outdoor noh stage, a revived Tensho-an tea ceremony room, a restored Muromachi Period (1338-1573) Meigetsu Gate and a strolling garden. Envisioned by Sugimoto Hiroshi, it took over 10 years since its conception to complete the project. Open to the public, it was designed as a forum to appreciate art together with the changing four seasons of nature.

(fossil cave), visitors left offerings of money, an ideological display of honoring the spiritual nature of the monument and be blessed from nature in return. In contrast, Western civilization was developed by conquering nature, but during the 10,000 years of the Jomon period, the Japanese focused their efforts in communicating and increasing their understanding of nature. The remnants of this belief can be seen from the number of words that defines different colors and the surrounding natural environment. There is no other language that equals the number of words like the Japanese language. Through those beliefs and the acquired ability, the Japanese have always felt the presence of divine powers in nature.

— So do you believe that such exceptional sensitivity had generated the uniqueness of Japanese art?

Sugimoto: Yes, and I think it is unique even within the history of Eastern civilization. I believe that the height of Japanese art occurred around the Fujiwara period (897-1185). *Mikkyohogu* (esoteric Buddhism teaching tools), which originated in China, had developed to the level of being works of art. Unfortunately, in China, Buddhism art had peaked and was declining, but the adaptation of the art developed and blossomed here, surpassing the artistry of its origin. During and beyond the Muromachi period (1136-1573), the level of craftsmanship, the pursuit of artistry had proliferated even to the common level. The quality of products such as dyed fabrics produced around that time are just unbelievable.

Recently, I've been collecting *noh-men* (masks used in traditional Japanese theatre). Actually, I have a good number of opportunities to collect them now. At first glance, many of them look similar, but if you look carefully, masks from the Azuchi-Momoyama period (1568-1603) and those from around the end of the Edo period (1603-1867) have a slight deviation. Such subtle difference is what's appealing about Japanese art, but at the same time, it increases the risk of counterfeiting. The only way to learn is to purchase things for yourself. I was an antique art dealer for about 10 years, but when I started to buy art for myself, the seriousness intensified by quite a margin.

Vajra Sword (vajra: Kamakura Period, blade: Yoshimits Ōno 2013, Lotus pedestal: Mitsukuni Takimoto 2013) collection of Odawara Art Foundation

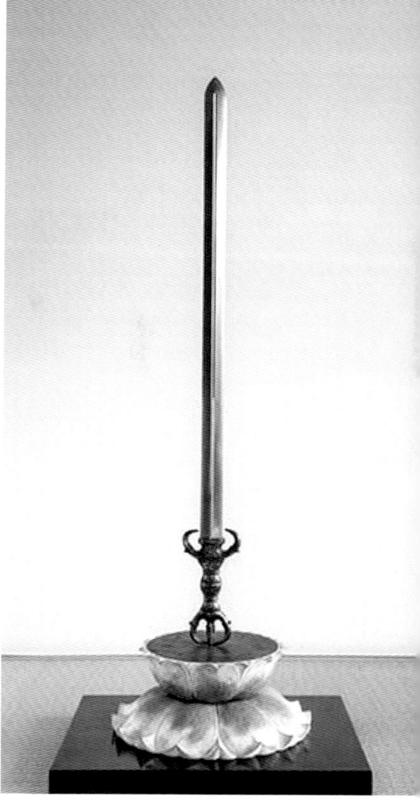

Sugimoto Hiroshi

A contemporary artist expressing his talents in photography, architectural design, sculpture, landscape design, theater, culinary and antique art collection. He moved to the United States in 1970 and has continued his creative activities both in Japan and abroad. He founded the Odawara Art Foundation, and in 2017, opened the Odawara Art Foundation Enoura Observatory. In 2019, he produced the performance as well as spatial design of the theater piece "At the Hawk's Well" at the l'Opera de Paris. He was designated a Person of Cultural Merit (Japan) in 2017.

自雪舟五代長谷川法眼等伯筆

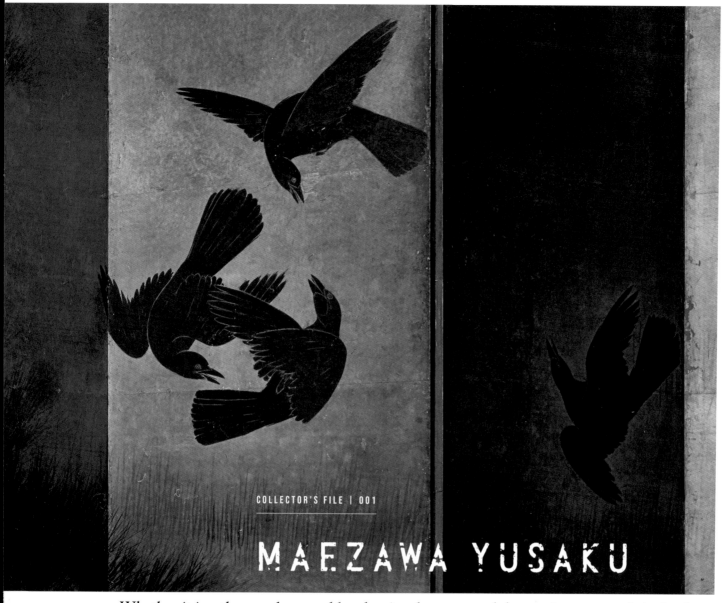

COLLECTOR'S FILE | 001

MAEZAWA YUSAKU

Whether it is a thousand years old or has just been created, beauty is constant. It is timeless.

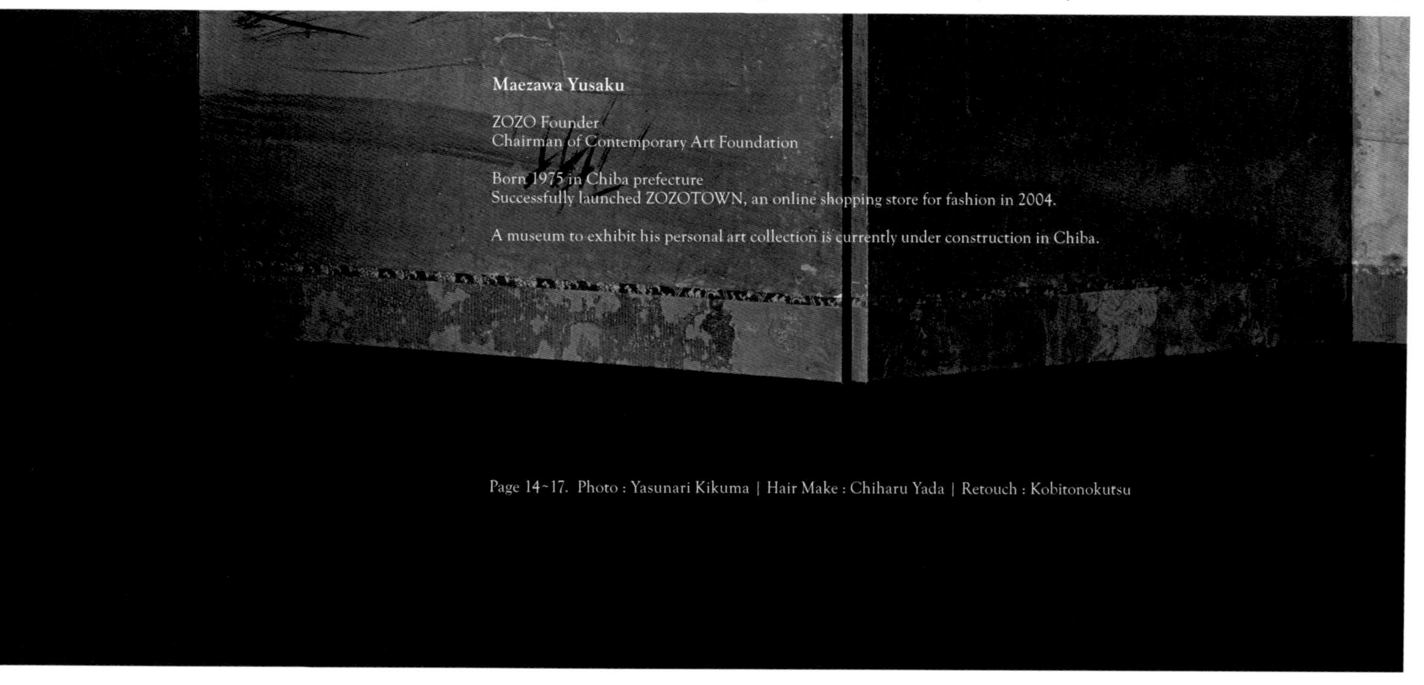

Maezawa Yusaku

ZOZO Founder
Chairman of Contemporary Art Foundation

Born 1975 in Chiba prefecture
Successfully launched ZOZOTOWN, an online shopping store for fashion in 2004.

A museum to exhibit his personal art collection is currently under construction in Chiba.

Page 14~17. Photo : Yasunari Kikuma | Hair Make : Chiharu Yada | Retouch : Kobitonokutsu

MAEZAWA YUSAKU

Yusaku Maezawa is currently one of the most famous Japanese people in the world. His road to success began in high school, when the band he formed scored a contract with a major music label. This led him to launch an online import record and CD business, which in turn led to expanding his business model into the fashion industry, where he founded ZOZOTOWN. This venture became such a huge success that it earned him a place among the world's richest people. Although his success story would make for a great manga series or movie, in recent years, Maezawa has become recognized more for being one of the world's most renowned art collectors.

Some of our readers will no doubt recall a story about him successfully bidding on Jean-Michel Basquiat's paintings in 2016 and 2017, both breaking price records for the artist's works. Maezawa's collection also includes pieces by Andy Warhol, Donald Judd and many other modern examples, as well as furniture, wine and super cars, some of which are displayed at his home and business locations. In 2012, he founded the Contemporary Art Foundation to disseminate the world of contemporary art and support aspiring young artists. Maezawa is currently the chairman of the foundation.

A few years has passed since we first heard that Maezawa was purchasing Japanese antique art. When we first contacted him for this interview, we were pleasantly surprised to hear that he was an avid reader of our magazine. He even offered us an opportunity to see the *Uro-zu*

Important Cultural Property: *Uro-zu Byobu*
(folding screen with paintings of crows and herons) by Hasegawa Tohaku
(Momoyama period, after 1605)

There is no reasoning to buying art.
If it moves me when I look at the art piece,
I will buy it. It's that simple.

–Maezawa Yusaku

Byobu (page 16), an extraordinary folding screen that he had purchased in the past, designated as an important cultural treasure, formerly part of the famous Kawamura Collection. *Me-no-Me* was granted with the honor of showing the masterpiece on its pages for the first time. After the photoshoot, we visited Maezawa's home for an in-depth interview.

"I'm actually renting this house so I don't go overboard with how I display everything..." said Maezawa, as he welcomed us into the home with paintings, sculptures and *objets d'art* hanging on its walls.

Immediately, we noticed fine examples of Oribe and Kenzan vessels, as well as white porcelain jars from the Joseon Dynasty and antique Buddha statues. Although the artifacts originated from various historical periods and

An assortment of Oribe ware. Clockwise from back to front: Five Oribe Boat-shaped Mukozuke Dishes, Ao-Oribe Style Shoe-shaped Tea Bowl known as *Cho-Ryo*, Oribe Hajiki Toy-shaped Incense Container, Oribe Hexagonal Sake Cup known as *Yotanho*, Oribe Tokkuri Sake Bottle, Oribe Square Dish with Handle

Contemporary and antique art, as well as antique furniture are all exquisitely displayed in the room. A white porcelain jar from the Joseon Dynasty was specially placed on the center table for our interview. When the subject of our discussion came to the topic of his favorite color, green, we were introduced to the Oribe and Kenzan wares.

regions, each of them were powerful and when seen together, appeared in a harmonious way.

"The very first painting that I purchased was a Lichtenstein. It was when I placed it on the wall at home that I realized that an artwork that I had only seen in a museum was right there in my home, in front of me. I became so excited I got goose bumps! That was more than 10 years ago, and my collection has been growing ever since," he said.

Maezawa personally directs how all of his art pieces are displayed, and he mentioned that he spent more than two days preparing this private showing of his collection to us. "I don't feel comfortable in open spaces. A big white blank on the wall makes me nervous. I've always been fond of antique furniture. That's why even with paintings and sculptures, I like arranging them in a set fashion. I feel very relaxed when surrounded by art," he explained.

When we asked why he started purchasing antique art, he gave us a unique reply. He said: "My house in Chiba has been under construction for a while now. In the basement of that house, I am making an authentic sushi counter. I wanted to use the best of everything, including all the dining wares to serve sushi. During my search, I ended up looking into

Left : Artwork displayed at the ZOZO office. The glass walled meeting room is decorated with works by Andy Warhol, Takashi Murakami, Bosco Sodi, Mai-Thu Perret and Jack Pierson. The room is also furnished with a Charlotte Perriand table and Jean Prouvé chairs.

Right : The CEO's office is decorated with Date Paintings by On Kawara. It is furnished with a sofa and coffee table by Pierre Jeanneret and wall cabinet, large table and chairs by Charlotte Perriand. Maezawa rarely enjoys them as he doesn't spend much time in this office.

*Below 2 photos were taken in 2018 at the time of interview. Maezawa has ceded his involvement with the operation of ZOZO at the time of this publication.

antique vessels and artifacts. Works by Rosanjin were especially tempting to use on a frequent basis. My favorite color is green so many of the contemporary arts and furnishing that I collected ended up being that color. I think the green shades of Oribe and Kenzan ceramics are awesome. In fact, the very first antique that I bought is the Oribe *tebachi* (Square Dish with Handle). The first time I saw the *tebachi* at Yanagitakashi in Kyoto, I was blown away. When they told me the price tag, I was again blown away! Although I never had any interest in the Azuchi Momoyama period (approx. 1568-1603), I immediately started researching it because I wanted to know more about Oribe."

According to Maezawa, reasoning never comes into play when buying an antique. He claims that most collectors are emotionally moved, fall in love with their newest purchase and then study the background and origins of their possession. "At first glance, the shape and decorations of Oribe ceramics are very simple and primitive, similar to contemporary art. I think it even relates to works from artists like Milo, Kandinsky and Lichtenstein. Perhaps some of the contemporary artists were

Top: Maezawa's living room: Natural light coming in from the open ceiling creates a relaxing atmosphere.
Bottom: Art displayed underneath the staircase leading from the entrance to the living room. (Photography by Kaoru Yamada)

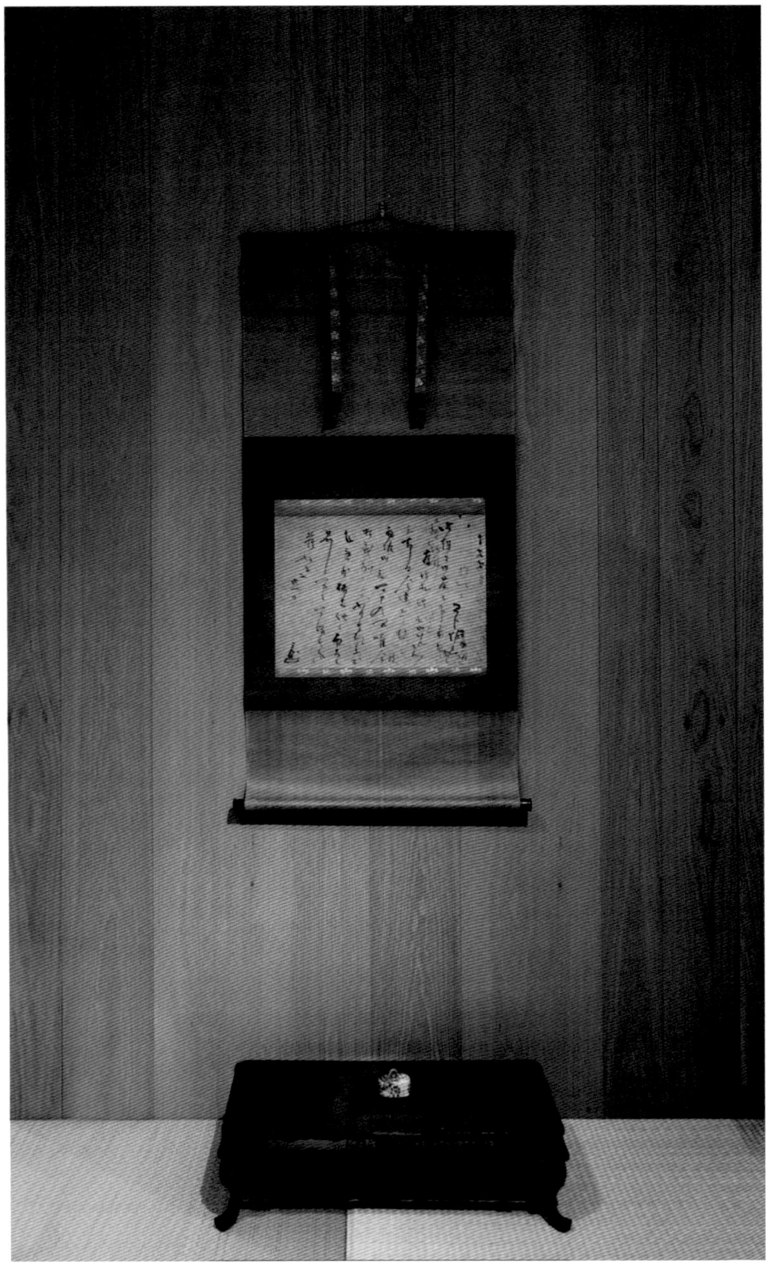

Oribe Shosoku (letter) and Kogo (insense container) paired up

influenced by Oribe. That thought alone has opened up the way I view things," he said.

As his knowledge base expanded, so did his interests, from food plates to teacups, leading to sake cups, flower vases and Negoro trays. "Right now, I'm very attracted to Buddha statues," Maezawa noted. "It's really becoming a habit of mine. Think about it, I can buy a wonderful Buddha statue for one tenth of the price of a Giacometti sculpture. I think Japanese antique art should receive more appreciation. Of course, I'll continue to purchase contemporary art, but it's not about being new or old. Ever since I was young, I liked mechanical things. That's why I'm interested in developing rockets and even planning to go to the moon. Perhaps I'm attracted more to the craftsmanship and the creativeness behind everything. I've also been thinking about trying pottery and learning the formalities of tea ceremonies."

Maezawa also mentioned that he is building an art museum near his home which is currently under construction. "It wouldn't be a formal museum of sort. Instead, it would be a place to share the art that I have collected as a hobby. If I can share the joy of art with the local people of Chiba and everyone else, it would make me happy."

An assortment of *Shuki* (sake cups), including Maezawa's favorite Oribe Rokkaku as well as Kizeto, Shino, Karatsu and Nabeshima. An attractive lineup for all fans of shuki. Even the shuki cabinet is fine art, a piece by Charlotte Perriand.

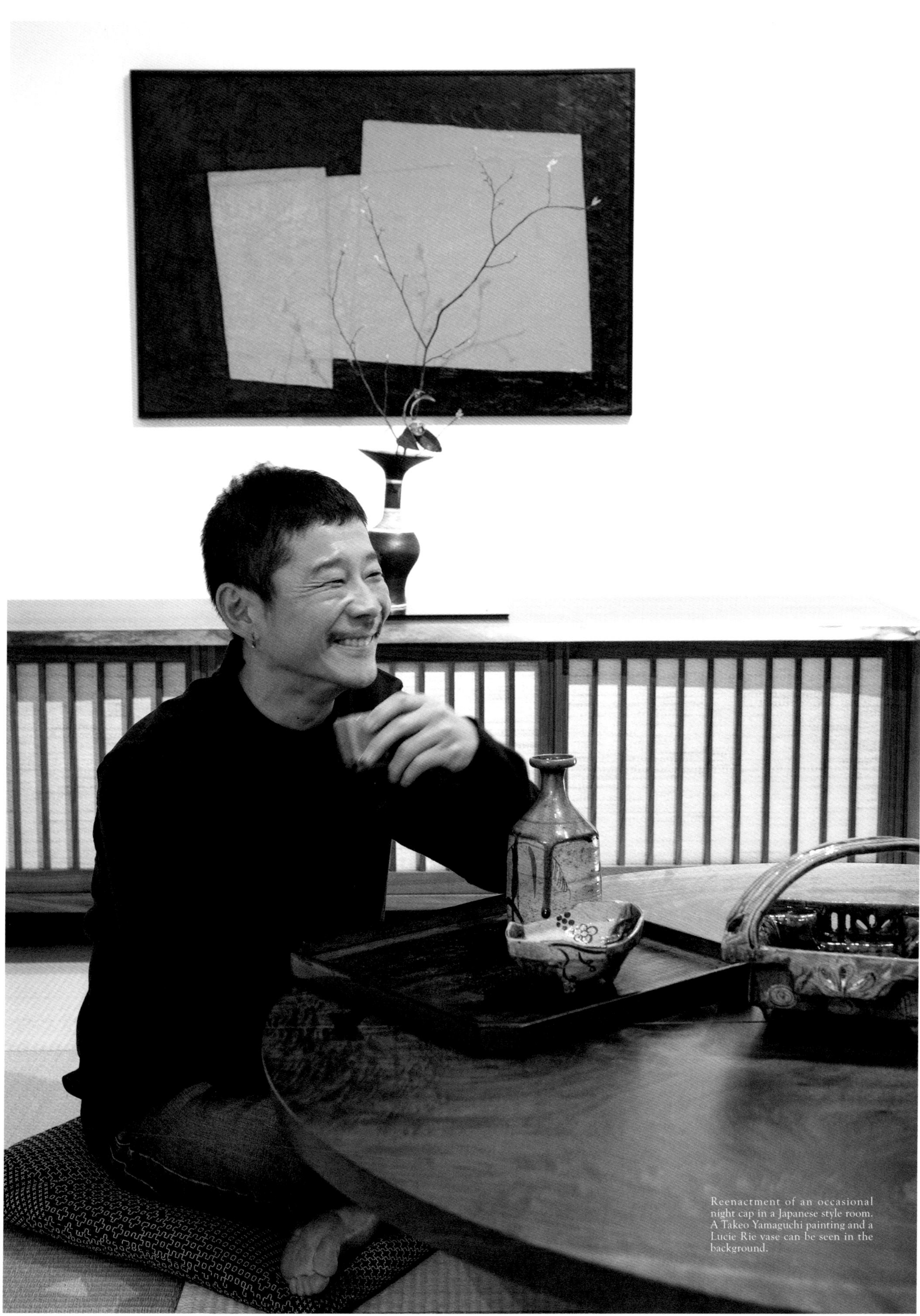

Reenactment of an occasional night cap in a Japanese style room. A Takeo Yamaguchi painting and a Lucie Rie vase can be seen in the background.

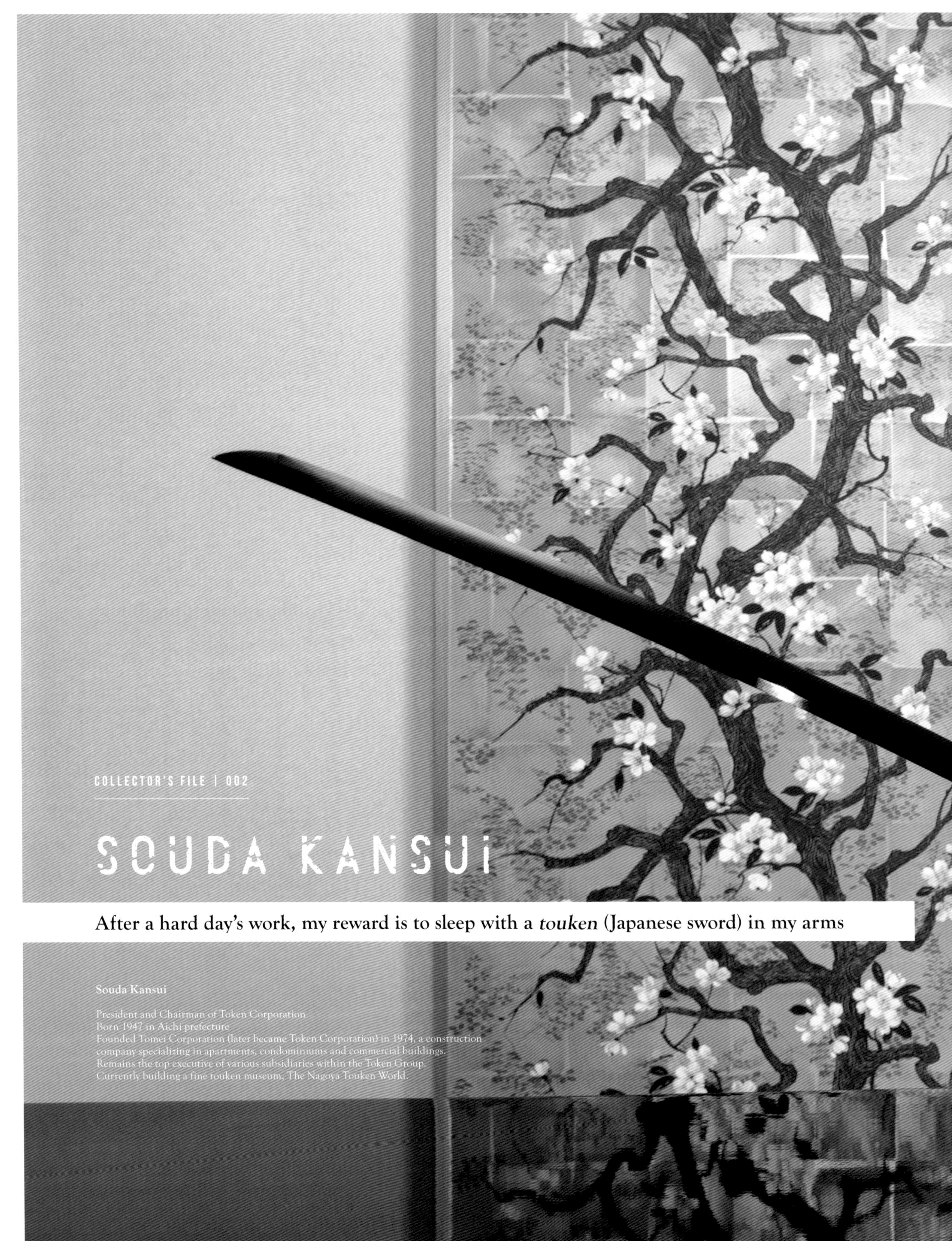

COLLECTOR'S FILE | 002

SOUDA KANSUI

After a hard day's work, my reward is to sleep with a *touken* (Japanese sword) in my arms

Souda Kansui

President and Chairman of Token Corporation
Born 1947 in Aichi prefecture
Founded Tomei Corporation (later became Token Corporation) in 1974, a construction company specializing in apartments, condominiums and commercial buildings.
Remains the top executive of various subsidiaries within the Token Group.
Currently building a fine touken museum, The Nagoya Touken World.

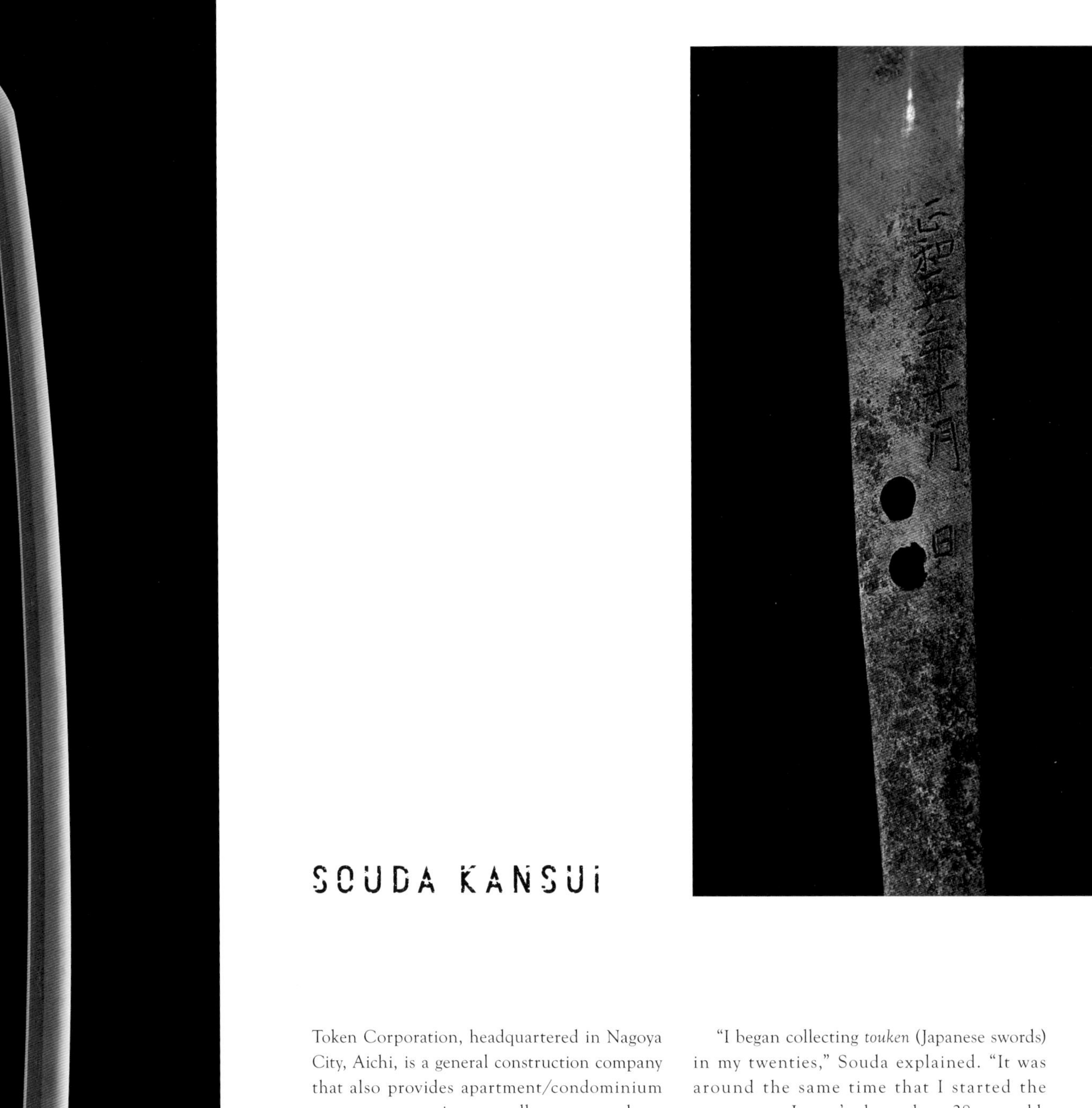

SOUDA KANSUI

Token Corporation, headquartered in Nagoya City, Aichi, is a general construction company that also provides apartment/condominium management services, as well as property lease amenities, under its HOMEMATE brand. With continuing growth, this blue-chip company has been led by one man since its inception in 1974, Chairman and CEO, Souda Kansui.

Aside from being a successful entrepreneur, Souda is an avid Japanese sword collector and has even appeared in a TV commercial for his company with a *katana* in his hands. When we requested an interview, he invited us to a golf club in Kuwana City, in Mie prefecture. The golf club, called the Token Tado Country Club Nagoya, is owned by his company, with his home located on the property. Some of his collection of Japanese *katana* and armors were on display in the club house.

Left & Top : Tachi sword—Signed by Bishu Osafune Jyu Kagemitsu Showa Gonen Jyugatsujitsu (October, 1316); Important Cultural Property.
(The tachi in Souda's hands on page 22–23)

"I began collecting *touken* (Japanese swords) in my twenties," Souda explained. "It was around the same time that I started the company, so I must've been about 28 years old. Perhaps I wanted an amulet of sorts as I began my journey in the business world. Just by chance, an acquaintance introduced me to a *katana* store in the outer borders of Kariya City, where I used to live. The place was just a barn house without a sign so I'm not even sure if it was actually a store. Although I've forgotten the exact location, I do remember that the inside was filled with *katanas*. I purchased a few *kuchi* (unit used to count swords), but nothing that expensive since I was still young and a novice collector. That first purchase included two Yagyu swords that were new and about the length of a *wakizashi* (short sword). Since one of them was light and easy to handle, it grew on me, and I kept it close by for protection."

Souda still possesses that Yagyu sword, which is now one of more than 300 swords in his collection.

Collection of touken (Japanese sword), katchu (armor) and teppo (rifle) displayed at the Token Tado Country Club Nagoya.

"There are many swords in my collection that are designated as an Important Cultural Property or former National Treasures. However, I feel that I am merely the current keeper of these treasures, and my obligation is to preserve them for future generations. A *katana* that I truly feel to be mine is probably only this Yagyu sword," he said.

There is no question that a *meito* (an acclaimed sword) has historical and artistic value. Nonetheless, the attachment and value that Souda holds toward the Yagyu sword is genuine, like a feeling toward a comrade which had stood by him as he navigated the world of business.

"I've always admired Japanese swords ever since I was little. My father's brother was in the Japanese navy and died in the war. I grew up looking at his portrait in the family altar wearing his white naval uniform carrying a sword. That is probably the origin of my admiration," he said.

The Souda family has a long history, dating back to when the family courted nobility in

Collection room at the ground floor of the head office building in Nagoya. Accessible to the public.

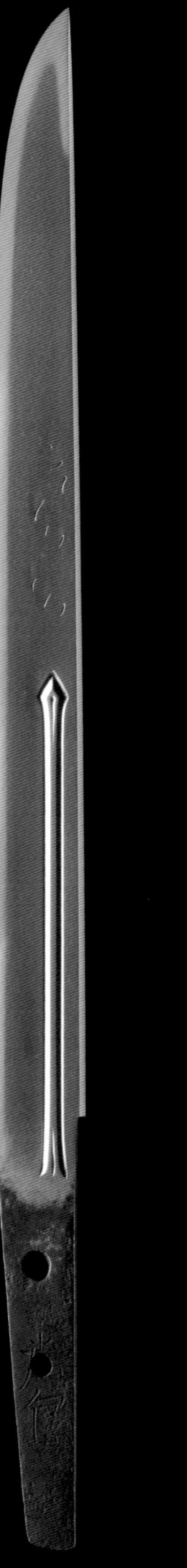

Tanto short sword - Signed by Mitsukage Enkyo Ninen Nigatsujitsu (Februrary, 1309); Important Cultural Property

Tachi sword - Signed by Bushu Shitahara Jyu Hiroshige; Classified as "Worthy of Preservation."

Kyoto, when the city was still the capital of Japan. The family then moved to Okazaki and owned a successful lodging business. Okazaki is where the famous *shogun*, Tokugawa Ieyasu was born. The city has historically been a popular stopover destination where many people, merchants and businesses passed through. Souda says that he had been greatly influenced in business by the way Ieyasu managed and ruled the country.

"When you start collecting Japanese swords, you soon realize that you cannot fully appreciate their value by just collecting," he remarked. "There is the *tsuba* (guard) and other accessories associated with the Japanese sword. Then you have the *yari* (spear), *teppo* (rifle) and *katchu* (armor) that were part of the period's weaponry. Swords that are considered to be *meito* have a story dating back to its maker and the warlords who owned them. Seeing their portraits and reading about them, your interest grows and makes you want to learn more. Just the other day, I was able to obtain a portrait of the warlord, Kato Kiyomasa, and a document personally written by Toyotomi Hideyoshi. One's interest just keeps expanding, such as collecting *musha-e* (*ukiyo-e* prints of warlords) and *gassen-zu* byobu (panel paintings of battles), which makes your collection grow."

According to Souda, this is how the project to build a museum, one that provides the visitor with the full experience and appreciation for the *touken*, started.

"We are building a seven-story museum in Sakae-ward, which is in the center of Nagoya City. The museum will be called the Nagoya Touken World and will have more than 2,700 square meters of exhibit space. It is scheduled to open in 2020, with permanent displays of more than 200 Japanese swords and 50 armors. The displays will involve VR and other digital attractions that visitors can enjoy using their smartphones, making it a fun experience for both adults and children. It's a theme park to have fun and learn about the Japanese sword. We spent many sleepless nights laying out the blueprints for this project," Souda said.

When asked if he had any regrets mixing business with his hobby, he replied, "No, not at all. I get obsessed with anything that draws my attention. This includes business, judo, which I started when I was young and which I now support as an official partner of the All Japan Judo Federation, and golf which I started in my forties and now own two country clubs. My company also hosts a men's professional golf tournament in Japan called the Token Homemate Cup. I enjoy the process of realizing ideas and concepts that come into my mind. *Touken* is the driving force that keeps me going in business as well as in my hobbies."

COLLECTOR'S FILE | 003

SATO TATSUMI

All that I have collected shall vanish like the mist, for in the end, I will give them away.

Sato Tatsumi

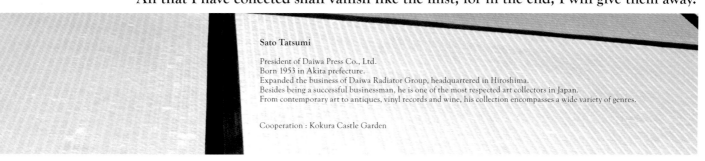

President of Daiwa Press Co., Ltd.
Born 1953 in Akita prefecture.
Expanded the business of Daiwa Radiator Group, headquartered in Hiroshima.
Besides being a successful businessman, he is one of the most respected art collectors in Japan.
From contemporary art to antiques, vinyl records and wine, his collection encompasses a wide variety of genres.

Cooperation : Kokura Castle Garden

SATO TATSUMI

Sato Tatsumi is without doubt one of the most respected contemporary art collectors in Japan. Mentioned every year as one of the top global art collectors in a U.S. magazine, he is perhaps better known outside of Japan. In 2017, Sato held an exhibition of his private Buddhism art collection titled *Shitsu-u-bussho–All Living Things Have a Buddhist Nature* at the Kosetsu Museum of Art in the city of Kobe. This exhibition left us with a very strong impression. When we heard about his plans to hold another exhibition in the spring of 2018 at the Kokura Castle Garden in Fukuoka called *Trace of Beauty–Sentiments toward Antiquity*, we immediately requested an interview. To our delight, he accepted and invited us to the Kokura Castle Garden, where he specially arranged a mini exhibit just for us in the shoin (study) and chashitsu (tearoom) of the castle. (page 28~31)

"Honestly, I am not good at giving presentations in an orderly manner. Today, I just lined up some of my collection hoping that you get a feel of how I view the world and the inclinations that I have," Sato said.

On the wall of the study hall, Sato placed a calligraphic scroll with the words fune (boat), written by Yamamoto Hisashi, an artist Sato talks about with glee. He also placed a potted plant from Kusamura, which is a flower shop that specializes in exotic plants. The study hall display was completed with a worn-out mayu (cocoon) plate placed on the opposite side of

Private collection display exclusively for this interview, in the shoin (study room) overlooking the pond at the Kokura Castle Garden (See page 32 - 33 for details).

the plant. In the tearoom, a scroll by Inoue Yuichi, with the word Hin (poverty), hung on the wall along with other items like the stone tools from the Jomon period (10,000 BCE - 300 BCE). Overall, the display space exuded a sense of strength, but at the same time conveyed a peaceful, placid atmosphere.

"Looking back now, I have been a collector of many things," Sato commented. "First, it was vinyl records, which I began collecting when I was about 15 years old. Beginning with rock music, I collected records from various genres. There was a record store called Merurido in Kichijoji City that I frequented. When I had the opportunity to speak with Ryuichi Sakamoto later on, I was surprised to hear that we had frequented the same record store back then. We had a good laugh when we talked about how I was buying one or two records per month while he had the resources to buy box full of records. This probably separated us in our final career choices."

According to Sato, this was about 50 years ago, when records were going for about JPY2,000-2,500 (USD20-25), which was fairly expensive for students. But he says that it was worth it because they represented something special. He also maintains that the record-collecting scene is still very deep and is one of the most intense markets around.

"The competition is much higher in that market. With antique art, collectors are usually at a certain age with some level of income, so there are fewer people to start with. But with records, collectors can be as young as elementary and junior high school students, all the way up to old guys like me. The energy of these collectors is very high, and they are quite persistent."

The subjects of Sato's collection began to expand when he was about 25 years old, as he started working. He developed an interest in quality vessels that he could use and began collecting contemporary items. Then naturally, he moved to older, antique items.

"Instead of getting deep into antiques, my interest made a leap to primitive art, such as sculptures that were bursting with energy from places like Africa and Indonesia. I think that was the turning point for me. From there, it was more or less a direct path to contemporary

Mayu plate made of bronze.

Sagamen (Saga mask).

Polishing stone and stoneware from the Jomon period (10,000 BCE – 300 BCE); former So Sakon collection.

art, and I spent a lot of time exploring that field."

When asked what about contemporary art appealed to him the most, Sato answered: "It's their strong personality, their uniqueness that contemporary art tries to express. To me, that makes them easy to understand and fun; however, I am starting to lose interest."

Sato cites that the lack of quantity is the reason behind his waning interest in contemporary art, and it is the reason he made the transition to antique art.

"Moriyama Daido (Photographer, 1938~), who I like very much, once said, 'There is no quality where there is a lack of quantity.' For example, with calligraphy art you have children taking penmanship lessons, and there are many letters, Buddhist scriptures and artwork. For more than a thousand years, there are countless works done by unnamed persons, and there are

At the exhibit hall of the Kokura Garden Castle.

also high quality scriptures from the likes of Kukai and Koetsu. In other words, quality is not born unless there is volume. Even Hiraoka Masaaki (Commentator, writer, 1941-2009) said that 'quantity is quality.' To put it in a Hiraoka-style expression, art is like a natural gem found from the vast ocean. I began to feel the urge to find that gem in the unmarked territory of the ocean. When you look at antique art from such perspective, the obvious prospects were either chadogu (tea utensils) or Buddhist art. I chose to get into Buddhist art since it can exist, even as a fragment. The ways of the tea (sado) cannot exist with one chawan (teacup). With Buddhist art, an encounter with a single statue or even a fragment allows you to indulge in the finest experience. The exhibition in the spring of 2018 at the Kokura Castle Garden was an opportunity to offer visitors with a glimpse of such world," he explained.

As we nodded in acknowledgement, Sato suddenly provided us with a unique perspective.

"Please don't misunderstand me, but in a way, Haibutsu Kishaku (historical abolishment of Buddhism) was a good thing in history. Of course, it must have been terrible for the people that were directly involved, but this event allowed high quality Buddha statues and Buddhist arts to be passed down to the masses. Today, we have the opportunity to see these fine works at museums and antique art stores, and to me, that is a blessing. In that sense, I greatly acknowledge the achievements of Masuda Donou (Entrepreneur, 1848-1938)"

Africa—Dogon tribe ceremonial tool for prayers; made with a staircase as its motif.

Portable hat in the shape of bellowed umbrella; made in China.

At the end of the interview, we asked Sato what he plans to do in the future. He replied: "Well, I am already 65 years old (in 2018), so I should be preparing to finish off my life's journey. Maybe I'll open up a rock cafe and spend time just listening to music that I like. In the end, I'm thinking about giving away all of my collection to friends that I know who will take good care of them. Of course, if I start running short on funds, I might sell them instead. I'm planning on drinking all the wine that I've collected. At the end, my ideal end is to vanish like the mist."

Sake cup with Camellia flowers by KENZAN
w 5.5cm h 6cm
Edo period
We are going to up for Special Triennial Tobi Art Fair 2021.

olding screen of wave painting
by Tosa Mitsuaya

Special Thanks : Ikenobo Headquarters / Nakanishi Shohoken / Shinmonzen Yanagi / AIC Akitsushima Kyoto
Photo : Akira Takemae

Breathing life into an antique

45th Generation Ikenobo Headmaster
Ikenobo Sen'ei

Ikenobo Headmaster Designate

Ikenobo Senko

Ikebana (flower arranging) using seasonal flowers is one of the core values of Japanese culture. The teachings of Ikenobo, the oldest and largest school of Ikebana, has embodied the art for centuries, and 2017 marked the 555-year anniversary since its restorer Sen'kei had arranged flowers as historically documented in the *Hekizan-Nichiroku* diary. For 45 generations, Ikenobo has passed down the aesthetic sense of Ikebana through the years, which is an incredible feat by and of itself. As an average fan of antiques, we imagine that arranging flowers with prized pieces would be an amazing experience, if only we had the skill and talent to do so.

Without irresponsibly taking matters into our own unskilled hands, we took advantage of an opportunity to make a special request to the current Headmaster-Sen'ei and the Headmaster Designate Senko, to show us the beauty of breathing life into an antique with their preferred antique vases.

Ikenobo, or even more so
Ikebana in Japan,
has its roots
in offering flowers to the departed,
To bestow a flower
is to bestow a prayer.

Ikenobo Sen'ei

(45th Generation Ikenobo Headmaster)

Flowers - Lotus (leaves and seed)
Japanese beautyberry / Japanese sweet flag

Flower vase - Negoro-Heishi (Red lacquer sake bottle)
Height 30cm / Muromachi period (1392-1568)

Arranging a flower to be offered to the *Omaedachi* of the *Nyo-irin-kannon-bosatsu* inside the main inner temple. Successive generations of the Ikenobo Headmaster have served as head priest of this Rokkakudo (Chohoji Temple, Kyoto).

Flower - Camellia Japonica / Amsonia elliptica

Flower vase - Sueki-Chokeiko (Long-neck vase of Sue pottery), Sanage Kiln
Height 25.5cm / Nara period (8th century)

Arranging flowers inside the Rokkakudo Dojo, an area only the Headmaster is allowed to bestow life to the flower.

Not at full blossom,
the half unfolding buds
represents the arousing energy of life,
An image held dearly
in the hearts of the Japanese people.

The Rokkaku willow tree
sways its branches
in front of the Rokkakudo,
A mythical willow where
Emperor Saga met
his beautiful princess,
A collaboration with a
Haniwa vase born of mother earth.

Flower - Oriental bittersweet
Ginger/Coral berry

Flower vase - Cylindrical Haniwa
(terracotta clay)
Height 44cm / *Kofun* period
(3rd - 5th century)

A popular power spot inside Kyoto's Rokkakudo Temple.
Arranging flowers underneath the match-making willow tree.

As scripted in history, Headmaster Sen'ei shoulders 555 years of tradition, but still manages to stand tall with a natural posture. Calmly entering the room, he began to inspect the flowers and vases one after another. Then without any sign of befuddlement, he started on the first arrangement. Unexpectedly to some extent, he occasionally conversed with the audience around him while he worked. He talked about the flowers and vases that were made available for the photoshoot and interview. He described the key elements of his creation as well as just gossiping with his staff. At first, we thought he was just trying to be as informative as possible to our editing team, but his staff revealed to us that this was his usual style of work. However, at the very moment when he was placing a flower into position, we sensed his concentration peak, as he focused his energy to the task at hand.

How did it feel working with the antique flower vases today?

I was just worried about damaging them!

We were happy your selection included earthenware and Sue pottery.

They are certainly not normally used in the world of Ikebana, but I tried not to disrupt the beauty of their original shape with flowers or leaves. The spout of the *Negoro-Heishi* and the outline of the Sue pottery are beautiful. I also gave a lot of thought into making use of the small opening on the cylindrical Haniwa.

How did you select the flowers?

Now we use everything, but traditionally there were some that weren't used. For example, rice plants were taboo. As one of the crops often celebrated for prosperity, it was forbidden to abuse the divine plant by snapping them by hand. Fruit trees, like apples and persimmons, which drop to the ground were deemed ill fated, so they were never used in celebrational occasions. Since Ikebana has its origins with priests offering flowers to Buddha, perhaps it wasn't acceptable to use anything that might invite any form of desire like an appetite. Also, anything with thorns were avoided.

Since we were using antique vases from different time periods in history, I wanted to respect the prosaic characters of the vases. The plants we use today are mostly grown in greenhouses. They are artificially grown to perfection. There's no distortion. The greenhouses provide moderate temperatures, light and nutrition but no wind. The beauty of naturally grown plants come from its harsh environment. The plant must endure whatever it's thrown at them from mother nature. That's why I used plants that were somewhat damaged, purposely bent or pruned of some leaves.

So there was a purpose to every detail.

Yes, and that even applies to the parts that are not visible. For example, when I was cutting the branches off, I did not cut at the base of the branch but left only a trace. It is the suggestive symbol of new life. The leaves that I pruned also feeds to the onlooker's imagination that it had been a source of food for life, an insect.

That is very interesting.

That is where Wa differs from western ideology. In the west, there is more thought into presenting a flower in its full blossom as a symbol of beauty. In the Ikebana of Wa, a bud or a half-blossom flower is used to invite the observer's imagination of his or her ideal blossom. In Ikebana, the shape and color of what you actually see is important, however, expressing the unseen image and the story of what's to come is the difficult part and at the same time most intriguing.

Flower - Pampas grass / Cattleya orchids Adiantum

Flower vase - *Seiyukokusai-Karakusamon-tsubo* (Blue glazed vase with black Arabesque design), Iran
Height 22cm / 13th century

Flower arranged by the window on the third floor of the Ikenobo Headquarters, overlooking the graceful tiled roof of the Rokkakudo Temple.

As the original form of Rikka,
Tatehana expresses the whole of nature
The entirety of Shinrabansho (universe).
Within a single vase,
let us begin
the enchanting ensemble.

Ikenobo Senko

(Ikenobo Headmaster Designate)

Rikka - Standing flowers / *Tatehana* - Standing flower arrangement

Flower - Urajiro (*Gleichenia japonica*) / Nishiki-gi (*Euonymus alatus*) / Okuroreika (*Iris ochroleuca*)
No-kon-giku (*Aster microcephalus var. ovatus*) / Silver cock's comb / Oyamabokuchi (*Synurus pungens*)
Chinese silver grass / Fujibakama (*Eupatorium japonicum*) / Brambles / Capsicum

Flower vase - Kodo Ryuji Hana-ire (Old copper flower vase with dragon handles)
Height 16.5cm / Ming dynasty

Rendering a stately dining table of a prestigious church. The Tatehana, arranged in an antique copper vase, enhances the empyrean atmosphere.

The vernal and scintillating beauty of roses,
Whether charm, elegance, kitsch or decadence,
There are no limits to the eloquence of flowers.

Flower - Rose / Baby's breath (*gypsophila paniculata*)

Flower vase - Ban Chiang Earthenware Jar, Thailand
Height 48cm / 1B.C. - 1A.D.

Lounge area surrounding a black brick fireplace. Roses arranged in antique earthenware adds elegance to the monotone wall and pastel upholstery staging a mysterious harmony

Light, air, water and time;
Elements that never stand still,
Meditation in action rules over that in stillness.

Flower - Toad lilly (*Tricytis macranthopsis*)
Asparagus / Japanese witch-hazel (*Hamamelis japonica*)
Red leaved rose (Rosa rubriforia)

Flower vase - *Shippo Araisomon Tsuribune Hanaire*
(Boat shaped vase with rough-waves design in cloisonné enamel), Nakagawa Joeki
Length 31cm / Height 15.7cm / Meiji period (1868-1912)

Poolside terrace with an abundance of sunlight.
Flower arranged in fishing-boat-shaped vase surrounded by the gentle sound of water and wind.

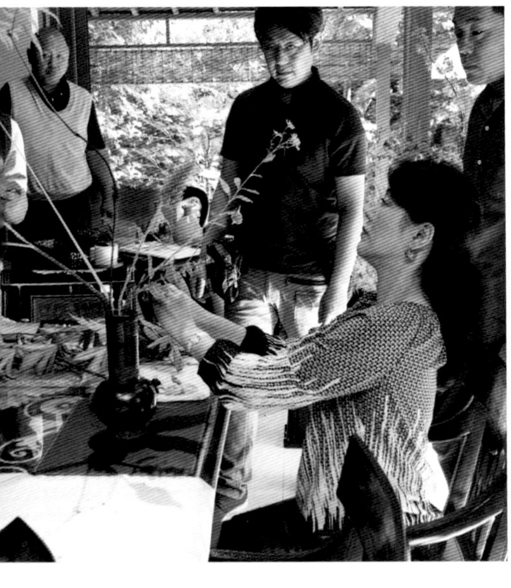

We requested the Ikenobo Headmaster Designate to arrange flowers for a modern western-style room. Despite having to work in somewhat of a restricted environment, she seemed to be enjoying the task throughout the photoshoot.

You started with the antique bronze flower vase. Was it *Tatehana*?

Yes, *Tatehana* is a basic style that was established before Ikebana was formally recognized. It tries to express the natural beauty of a standing tree and grass on the ground in a very simplistic style. The room in which the flower was going to be placed in today has a gothic style to it, with a strong assertion of its own principle, as opposed to a traditional Japanese room with a placid conservative atmosphere. I feel the colors of the flowers and how I had arranged them shows the vivid Southeast Asian flavor brought to Japan by the Europeans.

When you were finishing, you seemed to focus a lot at the base of the arrangement. Why was that?

Yes, in *Tatehana* as well as *Rikka*, the top part can be vibrant, but the base where the plants touch the edge of the flower vase must be tidy and sharp, otherwise it will affect the whole arrangement. Japanese Ikebana values a clear distinction between tenderness and sternness. I made sure that there wasn't any pause with my concentration until I finished arranging.

Perhaps that's why you seemed more relaxed when you started the second rose arrangement.

That might be true because the second arrangement was a *Jiyuka* (Free-style). Also, I feel roses have a special appeal that clears your emotions just by looking at them, so I enjoy working with them. I tried to use flowers with natural colors and bends that matched the soft texture of the flower vase. Of course, there are roses with brilliant red and pink colors with a strong presence, but I wanted to use colors that complimented the rustic beauty of the vase and vis-a-versa. I think the sofa, chandelier and the pastel colors choreographed nicely with the flowers.

In that sense, with the third arrangement in the fishing-boat-shaped vase for the poolside, I thought about the water and the green in the background. The flowers and the background appeal in concert with each other rather than independently.

It seems like you intentionally allowed the plants to overflow from the fishing-boat vase.

Exactly, I wanted to avoid creating a border between my work and the background. In fact, I wanted to bring in the background into the flower arrangement. As the sun began to set, the sunlight shined through the leaves creating an enigmatic effect that was really fortuitous.

How was it arranging flowers with antique flower vases?

I enjoyed it very much. At first, I thought that antique vases would have a strong sense of existence on their own, making them difficult to work with. I was pleasantly surprised that that wasn't the case, and I enjoyed the experience. Normally, I select flower vases so that its beauty comes together 100 percent with the flower. This time, I just selected the vases that I was simply attracted to. Then, I focused on how I could increase the allure of the vase with my flowers. I think the environment that I was in today played a big role. The weather was nice with a pleasant breeze coming through the window, the sound of flowing water filling the air and the rooms furnished perfectly. Compared to working in my usual atelier, all those factors helped me to work with a really open mind.

Flower - Amaranthus / Dendrochilum / *Chojiso* (Amsonia elliptica)

Flower vase - Naeshirogawayaki vase, Naeshirogawa kiln
Height 28cm / Edo period (1603-1867)

Japanese garden with a waterfall. Flower arrangement in the sunset.

Photos on P46-53 : Location provided by AIC Akitsushima Kyoto,
http://aic-akitsushima.com/

Past and Present of Antique Art

Through the years, art dealers have influenced collectors, molding the values of antique art with their assessments reflecting the times of history. With the dawn of a new Japanese era, Reiwa, and the ideals of the nation's population changing, one wonders if that would have any effect on the antique art industry. We spoke to the influencers of the *Kobijyutsu* (antique art) scene in Japan to hear about their past and present, as well as the history and future of the antique art industry.

FILE 01

TODA HIROSHI

TANIMATSUYA TODA

Born 1949 in Osaka, he is the 12th and current head of Tanimatsuya. For four years from 1973, he apprenticed at the Yayoi Gallery in Tokyo. He joined Tanimatsuya Toda Co., Ltd. in 1976, becoming its president in 1995.

Simple and primitive pieces attract him the most. Toda relies on his instincts across all genres. "Appreciating flowers and being emotionally moved by the scent of an incense are all part of training my five senses," he says.

The hanging scroll in the background is their family pseudonym *Ichigenan* (弌玄庵), written by Matsudaira Fumai.

A collector is something an antique dealer could never become.

On being born into the Tanimatsuya Toda, a 300-year-old family business

Toda: My father, Toda Shonosuke, married into the family and became the 11th head of Tanimatsuya. Initially, he thought marrying into the Toda family meant he secured an easy life, but that all changed when he saw the family's near-empty vault. When his predecessor died at 50 right after the end of WWII, Toda's family business was on the brink of bankruptcy, as the head clerk barely made ends meet. My father took over and saved the business. He was a very devoted father and often took me with him to many of his business gatherings; however, he never told me that I must one day succeed him with the family business.

I attended college, but quit after only two years, not being able to find anything in particular that I wanted to do. Then, I went to the U.S. and studied English for about three years. When I came back to Japan at 22 years of age with nothing really to do, I was immediately sent to Tokyo for an apprenticeship. I was initially supposed to go to Kochukyo in Nihonbashi, but unfortunately Kochukyo did not have a temporary apprenticeship program in place, so instead, I was sent to Yayoi Gallery in Ginza. Back then, my father told me that art dealers which dealt with paintings and other western art were handling much more business than those peddling *chadogu* (tea utensils), so he advised me to learn about this market. Yayoi Gallery was one of such dealers handling transactions of millions and millions of yen in western fine arts. After four years of apprenticeship, I joined Tanimatsuya in 1976. For 36 years until my

Tanimatsuya Toda's legacy overlaps with the history of Japanese antiques

Kuroda Taizo, White Porcelain jar

father passed away at the age of 88, we worked alongside each other, but he never tried to lecture me unless I asked him a question. He once told me, "If they give you a price that you think is way out of reach, apologize and decline the purchase. To retreat is also an insight." It was his way of telling me not to gamble on a big purchase and expect him to bail me out.

My very first purchase was a tea bowl, which was from Setsu Iwao, the late head of Setsu Gatodo. I also visited Kochukyo a lot. Once I asked for the price of *Jidai-Suzubuchi-kogo* (old incense box with tin edge) and it was much higher than I expected, so I had no choice but to decline the offer. That was a bitter experience that I can't forget, but now that piece is in our possession.

Enriching encounters : People and Art

Passing on the tradition of *chadogu* (tea utensils) is important, but I tend to like simple, primitive pieces that can be relatively interpreted without explanation. I think that mindset had been greatly influenced by my lifelong friend, Inaba Takashi, who is a collector of primitive art. He is the son of an *amimoto* (head of a fisherman's group) and married into a family that operated a *ryokan* (a traditional Japanese inn). Ever since he was young, he collected rare-looking shells and displayed them at his *ryokan*. It's obvious that he has a natural sense of design and style from the way he presents these shells. His natural talent was once recognized by Issey Miyake, who asked Inaba to design his vacation house. Through our friendship, I've been able to learn a lot from him. He is the one who introduced me to the ceramic artist, Kuroda Taizo. Becoming acquainted with the last head of the Raku family, Raku Kichizaemon (Jikinyu) is also something I feel deeply about.

In the past when I was displaying primitive art, people would say "That's only Hiroshi's hobby," but there is more to it than this being simply a personal hobby. Back when Rikyu was establishing the ways of the tea ceremony, it was considered art. In fact, Rikyu was already incorporating primitive art to his ways of the tea. For example, the *Sahari-Tsuribune-Hanaire*, shaped like a fishing boat used in the tea ceremony, is originally a copper bowl the Sumatra (Indonesia) used in various ceremonial and ritual settings. It was in the days of Rikyu when they reinvented the boat to be a hanging flower bowl.

The great divide of the Art Dealer and Collector

Life as an art dealer is quite difficult. It might sound like an excuse, but if gaining a profit was the sole purpose, it would be a crude profession. On the other hand, if you kept the ones you like and only sold items that you weren't attached to, you become a simple collector and nothing comes from that. It's interesting how the items that you are attached to gets purchased first. It's the destiny of an art dealer that he or she cannot keep an art piece forever. It's all about balance and if you're not wise in making the decisions, things can go terribly wrong very quickly.

Tanimatsuya has been in the *chadogu* business since the Edo period, so we have clients that dates back for generations. It's that historical background that I must always keep in mind and strictly abide by in my line of business. For the business and the industry, I cannot be a part of anything louche. I've become extremely careful with my actions. Although it may come as a surprise, even my father battled himself in deciding the right price when passing any of the utensils to a client. Sometimes, he would instruct me to change the price numerous times. He said that setting the right price is the foundation of our business. The price had to be fair on all accounts, making the client feel that dealing with Toda was always the best choice. That's why setting the price was always done with the upmost care and attention.

When the client is happy with the purchase, we can also feel blessed with the transaction. As long as we can maintain positive relationships with our clients, there's no business better than what we do.

Head of Buddha, excavated near Borobudur Indonesia

Oogikunatsume Fumai Gonomi (Japanese lacquer tea caddy with chrysanthemum design, favored by Matsudaira Fumai)
Hara Yoyusai (1769-1845/6)

TANIMATSUYA TODA

Founded during the mid-Edo period as a *chadogu* merchant in Osaka, Senba Fushimi. The founder's name was Sokei, who died in 1690. Successive generations went by the name Tanimatsuya Gonbei, abbreviated as Tanigon.

The fourth generation master

Gonbei *Kyuho*, died 1813 (Bunka 10)
As the trusted merchant to Matsudaira Fumai, the 7th lord of the Izumo Matsue Domain who was known to be a tea connoisseur, Kyuho delivered many masterpieces. In 1808 (Bunka 5), he received the title of Ichigenan along with a horizontal board handwritten by Fumai himself.

The eighth generation master

Rogin. 1843 – 1903 (Tenpo 18- Meiji 36)
Dealing with many masterpieces, Rogin was known to have had the sharpest eyes in the Meiji era. He was a trusted *chadogu* merchant to Fujita Denzaburo and Hirase Roko, both unquestionable connoisseurs in modern west Japan.

The 11th generation master

Toda Shonosuke. 1925 – 2012 (Taishō 15 - Heisei 24)
Born to an established *chadogu* merchant family, Ujiya in Nagoya, he married into the Tanimatsuya Toda family and succeeded in restoring the family business. He remains one of the most respected *mekiki* (connoisseur) of all time.

INFORMATION

3-3-10 Fushimimachi Chuo-ku, Osaka-shi, Osaka, Japan
tel: 81-(0)6-6231-5272

Seto Hafugama Chaire, Shibukamite-motouta, Chuko-meibutsu
Once possessed by Nakajima Soko (Choroan), disciple of Kobori Enshu, it was later introduced and possessed by Matsudaira Fumai. Box calligraphy by Fumai; uses *Yakutaishi washi* (Japanese paper) from Izumo as wrapping paper.

From right: Handwritten calligraphy of Jyudai (10th generation) Rosui on the box and the Ichigenan title sign, personally written by Matsudaira Fumai. Tanimatsuya business journal with a cover drawing of an *Ido-jyawan* drawn by Rosui. Published September 1935 (Showa 10)

の美

FILE 02

INOUE SHIGEO

KOCHUKYO CO.,LTD.

Born 1947 in Toyama prefecture.
Joined Kochukyo Co.,Ltd. in 1965.
President of KOCHUKYO from 2002 to 2019.

I'm still horrified whenever I make a purchase.
Between the tortoise and the hare, both the store and I are tortoises.
We take things slowly.
—Inoue Shigeo, Kochukyo

"I'm just one of the staff," said Inoue, while shying away from delving into his personal interests. After persistently asking him what type of antiques he liked, he finally opened up, telling us he preferred Chinese epigraphs. "I think bronze artifacts represent the basics of human creativity. When I retire, I'd like to explore the world of antique art from a different perspective," he said.

"I had no idea I was going to work for an antique art dealer."

It was Year 40 of the *Showa* era (1965) when I joined Kochukyo. The owner, Hirota Hiroshi, was originally from Toyama prefecture and had requested his alma mater for possible recruits. When I wasn't accepted to the college I wanted to attend, my high school referred me to Kochukyo. In other words, I joined Kochukyo because I happened to graduate from the same high school as Hirota. Knowing nothing about the business, I traveled to Tokyo to be interviewed by him. When we met, he only said, "You'll start work from tomorrow," and then gave me a place to stay on the second floor of the store.

Back then, the store wasn't a stone walled building like it is now, but a wooden structure with a large room to host private galleries and exhibits. At first, all I did was clean the floors and man the store when everyone was out. There was no training and the only instruction I received was to watch and learn. The customers that frequented the store were avid collectors with discerning knowledge. If I were to show them anything that didn't meet their expectations, they weren't shy about showing their disapproval. Those days were very stressful, but in retrospect, I was probably being trained by the best.

All our customers were imposing figures. A lot of them had been coming to Kochukyo before WWII. They often stayed in our store until very late, and that's when conversations sometimes took a lively turn. When that happened, the senior staff would leave everything to me and go home. Because I lived upstairs, I was always the one to remain and chat with the customers. Although I am not a great talker, I heard some interesting and valuable stories. When the conversations continued until late into the evening, the customers would order sushi and treat me to dinner. Those were good times. Most collectors are not very talkative, but they tried hard to collect insider information from me.

Learning the ropes on the job and accumulating experience

I was sent out on my first purchase by myself. At first, just having the courage to speak out at trade fairs was a challenge. Lacking knowledge and the eyes to determine what was good or bad, I initially looked for the Kochukyo signature on the outer box. My thinking was that if it had originated from our store, there was less of a chance of buying something that had no value. I am a natural worrier, and I was always worried about making a bad purchase or buying something for too much money; but to this day, I have never been asked to compensate the store for a bad purchase!

This one time though, I did make a bad purchase and was told to look at that item every day for the next four to five years so as not to forget the mistake I had made. Doing this is much more miserable than you might think. When I sold that product, it was the first time I got the opportunity to put that mistake behind me. When you get rid of a bad product, like selling something purchased by mistake, it is when you finally got reimbursed the money you had lost on the deal that brings a sense of closure. You know, you really understand the amount of damage that you created when seeing the actual loss.

Eventually, I was sent out to make purchases overseas. Back then, there was no internet nor were there smartphones. We made decisions based on seeing the actual product. Even if I called my store and asked for advice, they would tell me to make the decision on my own because they were not able to see the item. With most auctions, you only have a few minutes to make up your mind. The auctioneer is constantly studying the bidders and trying to get us excited. It is actually quite difficult to back out from a bidding war because, after all, backing out is like losing. That said, if the bids begin exceeding the items' fair value, backing out is very important.

The evolving Chinese and Korean art market

The influence of Chinese and Korean ceramics at Kochukyo is very high, and prices have been climbing because supplies are limited. I like offering our younger employees the same experience that I had, but things have changed quite a bit. It has become more and more difficult to find opportunities overseas. Even in Japan, chances of encountering ceramics that draws our interest have become rare. That's why I have been telling our staff to look more into Japanese art. Hirota, founder of Kochukyo, has always been handling Japanese ceramics. He was especially fond of *Karatsu* wares. I think we will continue to collect Japanese ceramics, but opportunities to purchase quality wares are becoming less frequent.

Fortunately, museums in Japan have a good collection of Chinese ceramics, but not many are in the hands of private collectors. In contrast, I think there are more Joseon Dynasty ceramics to be found out there. Perhaps the most frequently handled art pieces by Kochukyo are from the Joseon Dynasty. Compared to Chinese ceramics, minor scratches are not considered to be an issue, and

KOCHUKYO CO.,LTD.

May, 1924 (Taisho 13)

Founders Hirota Matsushige (Fukkosai) and Nishiyama Tamotsu (Nantenshi) opened an antique art store at Kanda Renjyakucho in Tokyo. They named their store Kochukyo, taken from an ancient Chinese literature.

1948 (Showa 23)

Reorganized as Kochukyo Co., Ltd. Fukkosai's nephew, Hirota Hiroshi becomes the representative director of the company.

1973 (Showa 48)

Builds the current four-story, one-basement company building.

INFORMATION

3-8-5 Nihonbashi, Chuo-ku, Tokyo, Japan
tel: 81-(0)3-3271-1835

Regulars of Kochukyo were all connoisseurs

they look proper in almost any setting. Since they can be appreciated all year round, many collectors grow a bond with their possession, making them keep them for a long time.

Establishing the standard as an antique art dealer

Chinese art pieces, whether they are ceramic or bronze, lose their appeal once their original forms are damaged. Although I cannot specify the reason, that is not the case with Joseon Dynasty ceramics.

Goryeo Celadon wares are somewhat similar to Chinese ceramics, while *Mishima* wares are somewhere in the middle relative to other Joseon Dynasty ceramics. In that sense, truly understanding *Mishima* wares is very difficult. A Joseon Dynasty ceramics collector once said, "*Mishima* ware is like music. The distinctive lines of *Mishima* represent each note." If one can learn to truly appreciate *Mishima*, it will become easier to develop an understanding for Cizhou kiln wares from the Song Dynasty (960-1279) or Japanese ceramics. That's why I've been telling our younger employees to expand their knowledge from the Joseon Dynasty wares, but they don't seem to understand where I'm coming from.

Going forward, chances of encountering quality pieces will become much less. It will become more and more important to take the time to study and make the right choices. In the world of antique art, the issue of authenticity is inevitable. Unless you are a genius, you will make mistakes. The most valuable lesson comes from making mistakes. That's why I tell our staff to go out and don't be afraid of making a mistake. However, the younger generations rarely take chances. Of course, we are not collectors, so we make our purchases using the funds from Kochukyo as a business, so perhaps being timid is a good characteristic in our line of business. Between the hare and the tortoise, we are the tortoise who likes to take things slowly. As for me, I'm definitely a tortoise.

KAWASHIMA TADASHI

MAYUYAMA & CO.,LTD.

Born in 1963.
Joined Mayuyama & Co.,Ltd. in 1988.
Assumed the post of the sixth president in 2017.

Price appraisal is important, but what is vital is to judge the true nature and the power of the works of art.
—Kawashima Tadashi

The Spirit of Mayuyama & Co., Ltd.

I joined Mayuyama & Co., Ltd. in 1988, which means I have been with the company for more than 30 years. Building a career in the art world was not my initial intention. Japan was in the midst of the bubble economy back in the late 1980s. By the fall of my senior year at the university, I had already received job offers from several companies, and I thought that I would join one of them. My major at Seijo University was Art Studies, and my graduation thesis was on Tang Sancai. Thus, antique works of art were not unfamiliar to me. Still yet, working at an antique gallery was not in my mind as a career choice at all.

However, when the second semester started in the fall, I was approached by Professor Higashiyama Kengo, an authority on Chinese cave temples, like those in the Dunhuang region. He asked me if I had decided where to work after graduating, and I answered that I had received several offers. Then he told me that a well-established antique gallery, Mayuyama & Co., Ltd., was recruiting. I suppose that he had some contacts at the company then. That was when I heard the name of this company for the first time.

Seeing that I had never heard of the company, the professor, who is usually a patient man, was obviously annoyed with my ignorance and took me to his office. He then showed me an elaborate picture book, which I now know as the *Mayuyama, Seventy Years*. The professor said I might have the opportunity to work for a first-class gallery that published such an excellent book. In the world of antique works of art, working for a reputable establishment was essential, he continued. As a college student, my image of an antique gallery was a

While overseeing domestic and international business including auctions, he is also active in research and promotion of field of arts, sitting on the editorial committee for *Tosetsu*, a monthly journal published by the Japan Ceramics Society. In 2017, he assumed the position of the sixth president.

little shady, but the professor insisted that I should pay a visit to the gallery so I just followed his advice.

When I visited Mayuyama & Co., Ltd. for the first time, they were holding a special exhibit of the masterpieces of Chinese inkstones, *Suzuri*. Thinking back on it now, it was an excellent exhibition of *Suzuri*, but being just a college student with only a little knowledge of Tang Sancai, it was a bit too advanced for me to properly comprehend. As I was making my way out, I noticed a beautiful ceramic pillow, *Tôchin* of Tang Sancai displayed in the corner. As I gazed at the impressive piece, a hand reached out from the side and picked it up. That was my first encounter with the then-president of the company, Mr. Takahashi Saburo. Feeling somewhat awkward because I was about to leave without properly extending my greetings, I immediately introduced myself. He invited me into a back room, where he gave me an interview on-site. He ended up offering me a job, and I accepted it as thinking that it would be great to work by leveraging what I had studied in college.

Difficulties in making the right choice

Immediately after I started to work, I realized that what I had studied in college was almost useless at work. Of course, I knew the basics about Tang Sancai, such as their historical background, their types of work, and some academic terminologies. Still, I had no clue about which was more valuable when they lined up two Tang Sancai works in front of me. Even if two pieces may look similar in appearance, sometimes their prices could be very different. Our job as art dealers is to see such subtle but critical differences. The policy at Mayuyama & Co., Ltd. is to select works of art based on their artistic values, not on their market values. It took me a while to grasp it. Even if you start to understand and recognize differences between look-alike pieces, that was not good enough. We need to be able to convey our findings in words. Thus, I learned everything from scratch, and to this day, I still find it difficult to find the perfect words.

In this field of business, nobody teaches you. You just watch and learn on your own. In my case, I learned through the daily operations. For example, I listened carefully to what the then-president spoke while helping him take objects in and out of storage or cleaning the gallery. I also carefully observed what he or senior colleagues purchased at exchange meetings, and then thought about what made them make the purchase. To put it simply, I just learned and gained from experience, not in theory. At first, I could not understand why people purchased works of art for millions of yen, but gradually, I began to understand.

Even back then as now, the company had a culture that would encourage academic approaches in the business, such as holding exhibitions, publishing catalogues, and writing expository documents. The company also possessed numerous rare and important books and catalogues from all over the world published in various periods of time. Many distinguished scholars and researchers frequented the gallery. I am fortunate to have joined the gallery having an academic atmosphere rather than focusing solely on buying and selling.

Jumping into the frontline of the business

When I joined, Mr. Takahashi, the then-president, was undoubtedly the pillar of the business. However, in my sixth year at the company, he suddenly passed away. Around the same time, one of the senior colleagues left the company to go out on his own, leaving only three of us to work in the sales department: Mr. Matsuda, who was in his mid-40s, Fujimura and I who both had just turned 30 years old. Since Fujimura and I were still inexperienced, we had no choice but to learn everything on the run as we desperately tried to keep the company afloat. Thinking back on that time now, many people must have been worried about the company's outlook.

In those days, London and Hong Kong were the main markets where we made purchases. Although it was often said that the fine classic collections were no longer coming out in the London market anymore, excellent works came on to the market from time to time. In Hong Kong, there were a lot of imitations, but we occasionally encountered some treasures. Since Fujimura and I did not yet have enough experience, we went for purchasing trips in pairs. I often went with Mr. Matsuda who was always reliable. There was another senior colleague mainly doing clerical work with whom I sometimes went for trips together. That was Ms. Iijima, the daughter of Mr. Iijima Isamu, who was the chief curator of paintings at the Tokyo National Museum. She was quite a connoisseur, thanks to her upbringing in which she had the chance to see many masterpieces. One time, when we were walking on Hollywood Road in Hong Kong, she suddenly stopped by an art dealer that seemed to sell nothing but imitations. She pulled out an object from the pile of junk and said that she liked it. So, we asked the owner how much it was. The owner, who knew what it was and its value, quoted us a price of a few million yen. Even so, Ms. Iijima insisted that I make the purchase. Despite feeling a little skeptical, I followed her advice and brought it back to Japan. Then, the piece was sold right away. Through experiences like this, I have come to understand that price is not an absolute index. Fine works of art have a certain quality or an energy from within, and that is what we need to instinctively recognize.

For the past decade or so, the market value of Chinese antique works has soared significantly as the Chinese economy grew. At one time, fluctuations in the market went so wild that our sense of the market price for which we spent several decades to accumulate became useless. Though it seems that the market has calmed down now, I think that the Chinese will continue to lead the market for a while. I find it interesting that sometimes an art work of high quality hits the market at a reasonable price, even in such market environment. It may be just differences in preference. Yet, if you focus on the genuine quality of the artwork, I think there is still an opportunity to build an attractive collection. It will become more important for the readers of this magazine and collectors to find a gallery or an art dealer who can be trustworthy and be comfortable with in making purchases to build a collection.

MAYUYAMA & CO.,LTD.

April 1905 (Meiji 38)

Founder Mayuyama Matsutaro goes to Beijing and starts an antique art business

1916 (Taisho 5)

Opens store in Ginza, Tokyo. Re-locates to the current location in Kyobashi four years later (Taisho 9)

INFORMATION

2-5-9 Kyobashi, Chuo-ku, Tokyo, Japan
tel : 81-(0)3-3561-5146

YANAGI TAKASHI

ORIENTAL FINE ARTS "YANAGI"

He was born in 1938 in Shiga prefecture as the second son of five children (four boys and one girl).
He helped his father's antique art store since he was a child.
In 1959, at the age of 21, he opened his own antique art store in Kyoto.

I learned a lot from all the mekiki (connoisseurs) that I become acquainted with.
–Yanagi Takashi

Shigaraki tsubo (jar) as a travelling companion

My father led an interesting life. He began his career as a normal white collar employee of Toray, but he decided to follow his passion and open up an antique shop in an area called Zeze in Otsu City. I often tagged along when he went to the market to purchase items for his shop. Because all of his four boys, including me, became antique merchants, I guess we naturally developed the same passion for antiques like him. You really must have passion for antiques to become a dealer. There are folks who decide to become dealers when they're in their forties or fifties, thinking that it's a good business to get into once they have some funds to spare, but these sorts of people don't last long. That said, if you are really passionate, you can start anytime.

It was Showa 34 (1959) when I came to Kyoto with my brother to start an antique store. I was 21 years old at the time. In the beginning, we handled anything that we could sell. Back then, large *Shigaraki* jars were actually hard to sell. My father used say, "Only small *Shigaraki* wares are good to sell;" however, they became quite popular, and we sold a lot of them.

There was this one man in Iga-Ueno who was a greengrocer by trade, but also handled *Shigaraki* and old Iga kilns as a hobby. I used to visit him every other month. He welcomed me every time I went, telling me, "I was expecting you to visit soon." Most of the time, I ended going home on the train with large antique jars

When we visited Antique Art Yanagi, the shop was in the midst of arranging flowers– *hanamomo* (hana peach) and *tsubaki* (camellia japonica) in a flower vase called *tanba* (Japanese pottery originating from Hyogo prefecture)–for display in the store.

The arranger was a lady named Kawashima Nachiko, who took over the flower-arranging duties after Sadako-san, the wife of Yanagi Takashi, passed away. Kawashima, who had been a good friend of Sadako-san, as they shared a mutual love for flowers, has in fact even published a book on the subject, titled *Flowers Through the Days – The Art of Flowers in the Yanagi Antique Gallery*.

As we watched Yanagi gently looking on as the flowers were being arranged, we had the mystifying feeling of being an intruder to a precious ritual.

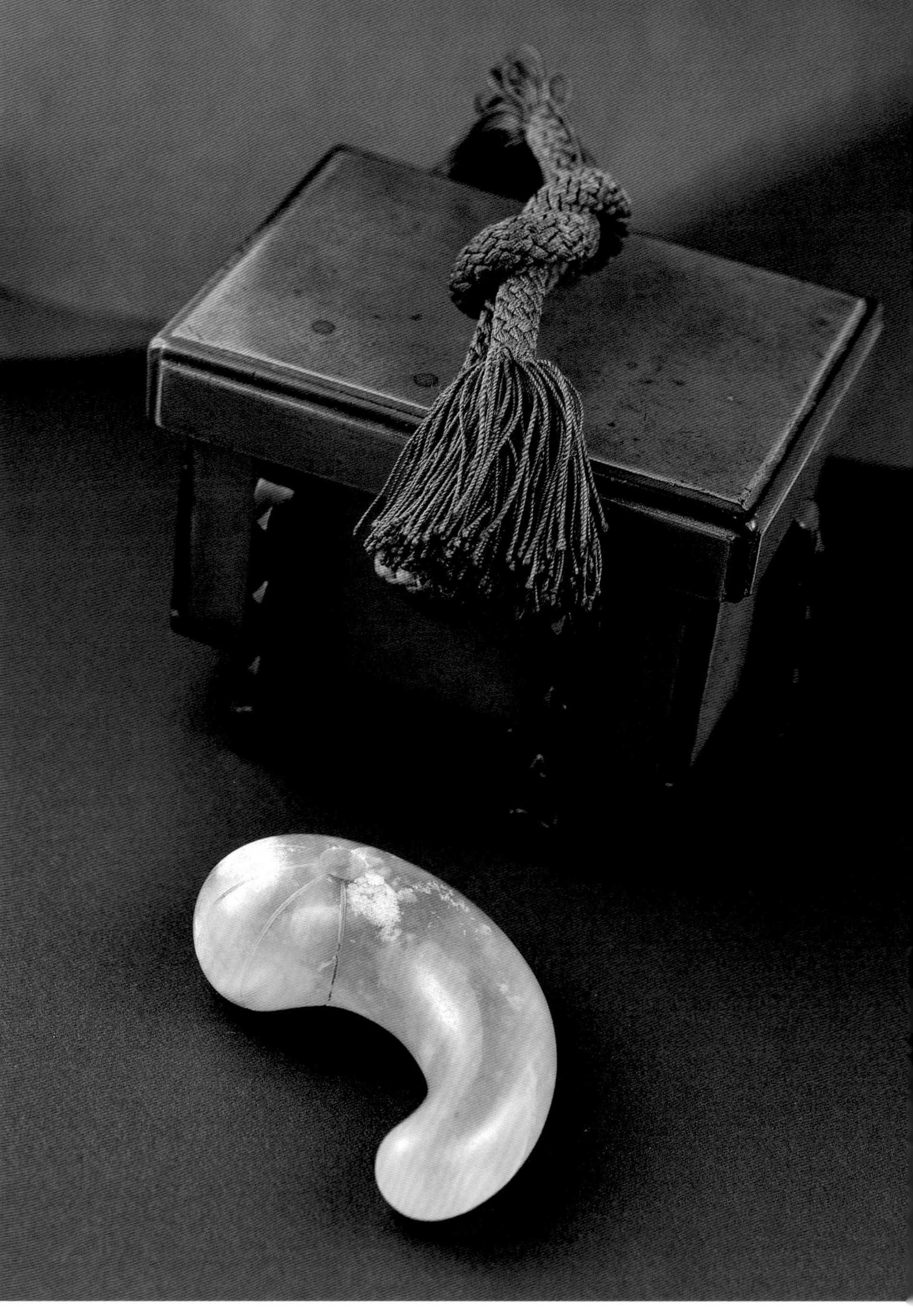

Magatama
Kofun period (Tumulus; 250-552)
Length: 7cm

in both hands. It was a workout just carrying them back, but my rapacity for wares won over every time. I definitely visited that place a lot.

Learning from the Mekiki (connoisseurs) clients

It was Showa 41 (1966) when I opened the store on Nawate-dori. It has been 50 years now, and the time has passed by very quickly. When we first opened, there weren't many antique stores on the street like there are now.

The renowned Shirasu Masako frequented our store from the time we first opened on Higashioji-dori. She often said, "Unless the wares can be used, they are not interesting." The literary critic, Kobayashi Hideo, initially came with Ms. Shirasu, and then began frequenting the store on his own. Kawabata Yasunari, the winner of the Nobel Prize for Literature, was an avid collector, and when he liked something, he bought it without even asking the price. He is often thought to be a difficult or a hard person to approach, but he was actually very gentle. Even my kids were attached to him. He would often call to my sons and write something for them as a lesson.

The philosopher, Tanikawa Tetsuzo, was an interesting gentleman. He knew exactly what he liked and what he didn't like, and immediately moved the items that he didn't like to the side.

All these renowned clients weren't overly specific about what they wanted, but they knew a good piece of art when they saw one. I was able to learn a great deal from them. They weren't too keen on items that were obviously of high value such as *chadogu* (tea utensils), and even if they didn't know much about a specific item, they were open to hear my explanation, which often led to them purchasing it.

Buddhist Art

There were also many customers that liked Buddhist art. Hosomi Ryoichi, who went by the pseudonym Kokoan (1901 – 1978), liked many things, but he especially liked Buddhist paintings and *Rinpa*-style paintings. He was a true connoisseur with tremendous knowledge. I'm sure many people were influenced by him. Right now, the collections are all at the Hosomi Museum, but in the old days, his collections were kept in the family vault, and he would go inside to select a piece to bring out.

I have a bitter, regretful experience with *Mikkyo Hougu* (Esoteric Buddhist ritual object). There was this wonderful large *gokosho* (five-blade varja) from the Heian period (794-1185). I really wanted to make the purchase, but I hesitated. When Kitamura Kinjiro (1904-1991) saw it, he immediately bought it. He sure had an eye for something good. The piece is now at the Kitamura Museum. It is a masterpiece and having a chance to buy it was an opportunity of a lifetime. It was something I will probably regret for the rest of my life.

It's not fun unless it comes out in the open

There have been many items that have come my way, but if I was asked to list my favorites, I would say currently, they are magatama (ancient comma-shaped bead) and Buddhist paintings. I also like stones. In the past, I handled many Buddha stone sculptures and stone pagodas.

There is nothing like an Imperial Jade with a good color shade. Jade pieces are still a very difficult genre to understand because there are many mysteries surrounding them, but that's what makes them fascinating. There are many collectors of *magatama*, like Kano Jihei, the 7th-generation president of Hakutsuru Sake Brewery (1862-1951), who erected the Hakutsuru Fine Art Museum. Many antique art collectors end up becoming *magatama* collectors. As for Buddhist paintings, the appeal is the number of great paintings out there, but they don't appear in the open market too often. It's not fun unless they come out in the open, but a good painting in good condition is very hard to come by.

It's rare when I regret not making a purchase. When you start worrying about making a mistake, you start missing all the good deals. You learn the most by making mistakes. If I were to give some advice to anyone who might be starting an antique art business, I would say to them, "Don't let the price scare you. Be committed and make the purchase." After all, if you don't buy it and own it, you will never understand the true value of that artwork.

ORIENTAL FINE ARTS "YANAGI"

1959 - Opens store at Higashioji, Kyoto

1966 - Moves the store to Gion-Shinmonzen

1968 - Re-opens store at the same location

INFORMATION

195 Nishinomachi, Higashiyama-ku, Kyoto
tel : 81-(0)75-551-1284

FILE 05

TAJIMA MITSURU

London Gallery

Born in 1936 in Fukui prefecture.
Influenced by his father, he became familiar with antique arts from an early age.
In 1955, after graduating high school, he went to work for Jintsu Seigando in Tokyo.
After one year, he decided to become independent.
Traveled to the U.S. in 1963.
Opened his own antique art store, the London Gallery, in 1969.

A sudden encounter with the crossroad of life

After graduating Fujishima High School in Fukui, I came to Tokyo to work for Jintsu Seigando, but I ended up leaving the job after only one year. An acquaintance of mine, Mr. Kenji Yoneyama, who was the owner of a printing company and an avid antique art collector, planned to open an antique art store with a man named Hata Hideo, who served as the model of a character depicted in the novel Chinpindo Shujin written by Ibuse Masuji. They both wanted to hire a young storekeeper, and they thought I would be a great candidate. But when they offered me the job, I had just started at Jintsu at the time, so I asked them to give me a year to gain experience. One year later, I officially left Jintsu Seigando to join the new venture; however, by that time, the two men had an argument and had split up. They opened their own independent stores, and I was offered a position by both men, but I decided to go with Mr. Yoneyama. Thinking back now, that was a sudden encounter with a crossroad of my life.

We opened up a small shop in Tomoecho. The store was less than two meters wide and two meters deep. Tomoecho, now known as Toranomon, had about thirty antique art stores back then. Yabumoto, which was already a well-

When I turned 50 years old,
I decided to only handle art pieces that I liked.
—Tajima Mitsuru

"I buy items that I like and have personal use for them, even if we don't handle such items in our store." He keeps a brush case made of koyori (twisted paper strings) from the Joseon Dynasty period (1392-1897) by his side.

established antique art store was located just down the road, so many of its customers ended up visiting our store. Since Mr. Yoneyama published many books written by the Shirakaba-ha writers, he was friends with a lot of them. Shiga Naoya, along with many other writers, were into antique art so they frequented the store. Interestingly, Hatasegawa-zeki, often referred to as the God of Sumo, was also a regular at our store.

We handled everything, but because I liked Shoki Imari and artifacts from the Joseon Dynasty, we carried a lot of ceramic wares. Mr. Yoneyama liked Buddhist art and Rinpa style arts. Back then, works by Kenzan were still fairly easy to come by. Once, we also sold an oil painting by the French artist, A.Maillol, to Shiga Naoya.

Antique art has its trends, and back then, works that were relatively rough in appearance were popular, rather than the finely detailed arts that's popular today. If we were to reference antique wares from the Joseon Dynasty, those that were uniquely disfigured were preferred over the beautiful underglaze wares produced at the official kilns of the Joseon Dynasty. In other words, the style of work that Yanagi Muneyoshi liked was more popular compared to the works preferred by Ataka Eiichi. There were more antique art enthusiasts back then and more people wanting to sell antiques, so there were more opportunities to buy them. I

Wucai Zun Vase with Dragon and Flower design
Wanli mark and period(1573-1620)
A masterpiece of Banreki Akae, Wucai Zun Vase, brought back from Paris by Tajima

was first introduced to Shirasu Masako by Koyama Shigeru. When Ms. Shirasu wanted something that happened to be rather expensive, she would say, "Hey, take this with you," and handed me something from her collection. The antiques that she told me to take were popular items that sold well in the market, so I often hesitated to take them.

Rare finds overseas

After about three years, we moved our store to Roppongi. I believe I was about 22 years old when I met Harry Packard. Mr. Packard was an art collector and a researcher. In order to finance his collection, he took the time and effort to travel all around the United States and Europe, selling and buying antique arts. Otherwise, it would have been impossible to build the collection that he had. Ultimately, he sold half of his collection and donated the other half to the New York Metropolitan Museum. The donation significantly increased the level of Japanese art at the museum.

One day, Mr. Packard invited me to join him on a trip around the United States. We visited cities like San Francisco, Santa Barbara, Los Angeles and San Diego. Influenced by my father, I liked native and primitive art, so I found a lot of interest in Native American arts such as their dyed artifacts.

Banreki Akae, Chinese masterpiece

A little while after, I attended the Eckersley School of English in Oxford to learn English. There, I became friends with a French girl, who told me that her house in Paris was full of ceramic wares from China and invited me to visit. She lived in a nice house near the famous Arc de Triomphe. The house was full of Chinese ceramics, and I noticed a Banreki Akae vase (Wucai Zun Vase, Chinese ceramics from Wanli period, 1573-1620) modified into a lamp complete with a shade. It was popular to modify ceramics into interior furnishings, even by making holes and other unrestorable modifications. Luckily, this vase had not been altered to such an extent. I told her that the vase was something of value and suggested to be stored in a safe place. After my visit to her house, she gave me a call and said that I can buy the vase. I was so excited to receive the offer. On my way back from Europe, I took a detour to the U.S. and visited the Museum of Fine Arts in Boston. There, I made a thrilling discovery: There was an identical vase on display. These kinds of vases are usually produced in pairs, so I immediately knew that they were originally a set.

Can't stop what you love

During my initial years in the business, I was doing whatever I could to keep going, but when I turned fifty, I made the decision to only deal in things that I truly liked. I wasn't going to be concerned with making a profit but wanted to focus more on subjects that I had a passion for.

I don't think there's anyone else that has handled a broader variety of items than I have. I've dealt with katanas (Japanese swords), yoroi (Japanese armors), ukiyoe (Japanese woodblock prints and paintings) and various other items. I have organized countless exhibitions. It's quite interesting how many stories can be produced by focusing the exhibition on a single antique art theme. I have also published many pictorial archives.

It has been about 20 years since I began focusing on Buddhist artwork. Before, there were many antique arts stores handling both good and bad antiques at the same time. You needed a pretty good eye to do any business with them. Now, there are many exhibitions that allows you to actually see truly valuable antiques. Many of the younger antique art merchants have come a long way in advancing their knowledge from such opportunities. What I found is that you must own an item for a long time to really appreciate its value. At times, you might realize your own shortcomings. Of course, you can't make too many mistakes. Looking back, there were more items on the market so there were more opportunities to make mistakes and learn from them.

Back in the day when I visited San Francisco, there was an antique art merchant by the name of Harry Neal and he said, "You guys came a bit too late. There's not much to buy here anymore." I thought that was strange because we ended up buying a lot from him. I find it funny that I'm now saying similar things to people younger than me. Perhaps they will be able to find new value in things. When you become passive, things will only retrogress. I think I should be retiring, but you can't stop doing what you love. I will probably be doing what I love forever.

London Gallery

1969 Established the London Gallery in Roppongi, Tokyo
2009 Opened the Shirogane Gallery

INFORMATION

6-6-9 Roppongi, Minato-ku, Tokyo, Japan
tel : 81-(0)3-3405-0168

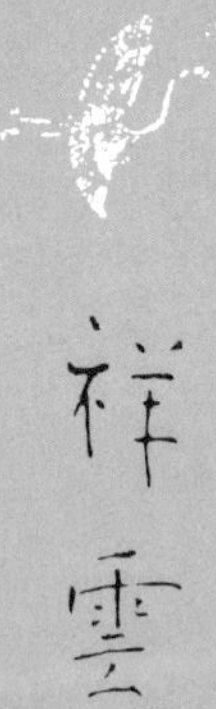

Shishi and Komainu (Guardian Lions)
Kamakura period, 12th century
Wood
Komainu: H. 85 cm
Shishi: H. 84 cm

Art Hotel
ART MON ZEN KYOTO

391,Motomachi,Furumonzen-dori,Higashiyama-ku,Kyoto 605-0089,Japan
Tel +81(0)75-551-0009
info@amz-kyoto.jp
www.amz-kyoto.jp/en/

Fine Art
NAKANISHI SHOHOKEN Co.,Ltd

388-1,Motomachi,Furumonzen-dori,Higashiyama-ku,Kyoto 605-0089,Japan
Tel +81(0)75-551-8000
www.kyoto-nakanishi.com/en/

Sometsuke Sansuimon Ōbachi (Shoki Imari Porcelain Blue and White plate with landscape design). Diameter: 44.5cm, Height: 10.0cm c.1630 - c.1640, Edo period Private collection

Dressing up KOIMARI

Main Dish=KOIMARI, ordinarily, a chef picks a plate to match the cuisine. This time, we picked the plates and requested to be served with a cuisine to match. Japan's first rate chef serves us *Shoki Imari*, *Kakiemon* and *Nabeshima* with fine cuisine to complement these wonderful examples of *Koimari* masterpieces.

Porcelain Commentary: Suzuta Yukio (Director of The Kyushu Ceramic Museum)
Chef: Hirose Kazuhiko (Kaiseki Ichimonji)
Special Cooperation: Iketani Masao (Ikemasa)

KOIMARI (Old Imari)

Porcelain made in the Arita area of Saga prefecture is called *Aritayaki*. The name *Imariyaki* derives from the port name, Imari Harbor, where the porcelain ware was shipped off from the region. In accordance to its production year, process and various other factors, these porcelain pieces are categorized as *Shoki Imari*, *Kokutani* style, *Kakiemon* style and *Kin-ran-de*. There is also a separate lineage called *Nabeshima* style, invented by the Nabeshima clan that boasts the finest quality. In this article, the term *Koimari* will be used to include all of the examples mentioned above.

Great Dragon Lobster in Paradise

We were speechless when this large porcelain plate was presented in front of us. We were told it was big, but we did not expect something quite this large. It was also deep.

"Isn't this great!? It's owned by a dedicated *Koimari* collector, and it is the largest of his collection. He's been collecting for decades and thought he had seen it all, but when he encountered this plate, he was awed. The world of antique art is truly profound," said Iketani Masao, who kindly arranged the plate for this article.

The chef, Hirose Kazuhiko, had to completely rethink the menu after seeing the large *Koimari*. "I was going to make a *Hassun* style dish, but after seeing this very large and deep plate, I needed something that wouldn't look out of place on this masterpiece," he explained, so he decided to prepare a giant Japanese spiny lobster in *Shiraga-mori* style.

The dish turned out to be perfect for festivities, a celebrative Japanese spiny lobster symbolizing longevity dancing in paradise.

The Porcelain

Adorned with the brilliant blue from gosu (zaffer), this plate features a deep conclave surface that would have been praised as a vessel of any delicious offering. The large rim of the plate has been detailly shaped as a garland. The dynamic brush strokes of the underglaze and its size resembles the large plate owned by the Museum Yamato Bunkakan in Nara that has been designated as an important cultural treasure. Large plates of *Shoki Imari* had traditionally been made at the Yanbeta kiln in Arita, and this plate seems to have originated from there. Many similar plates of this size were produced from the 1630s to well into the 1640s. The darkness in shade of the *gosu* blue often determined the value of the porcelain. The base is rather small with some trace of sand around its glazed edges. As often found on *Shoki Imari*, there are a few finger marks on the *kodai* (base) left from the glazing process.

Dish : Japanese Spiny Lobster Shiraga-mori style

After boiling the lobster, the tail meat was removed with the white portion delicately hand-shredded into a fine flake. Flavored with a pinch of salt and lemon, the meat was sprinkled with broiled sea urchin powder for added aromatic flavor and served with Tokyo grown wild turnip and spinach.

Flowers of Genroku blossoms with colors of spring

"My dear sister, I smell something good."

"Today is the *Joshi-no-harai*, *Momo no Sekku* (Girl's festival). They are celebrating our reunion after 300 years. Look, look over there at the delightful feast."

You can almost hear this conversation take place between the sitting figurines.

According to Iketani, seeing two sitting *Kakiemon* figurines together like this was a rare opportunity.

"These ladies made their trip back from Europe to Japan separately," he explained. "They look identical so it should be safe to assume that they are sisters from the same kiln. To match the figurines, we brought a large *Kakiemon*-style *Hanamon* (flower) porcelain plate. Don't you think the plate design has a somewhat western feel to it?"

"Because it is the *Momo no Sekku* season, I'd like to prepare *chirashi-sushi*," chef Hirose commented as he began preparing the classic Japanese cuisine.

Then, the porcelain plate from the luxuriant culture of the *Genroku* era (1688-1704) appeared in front of us without any fade to its original vibrant colors.

The Porcelain

Four kinds of flowers—chrysanthemum, plum, camellia and peony—are drawn in subdivided compartments in a radiant pattern. A boldly placed image of the peony in the center establishes balance to the entire design of this truly artful porcelain plate. When the plate is full, most of the drawing hides underneath the food and, as the dining progresses, the peony exposes its elegance.

This subdivided radiant pattern is similar to the *fuyoude* style; however, the borders on this

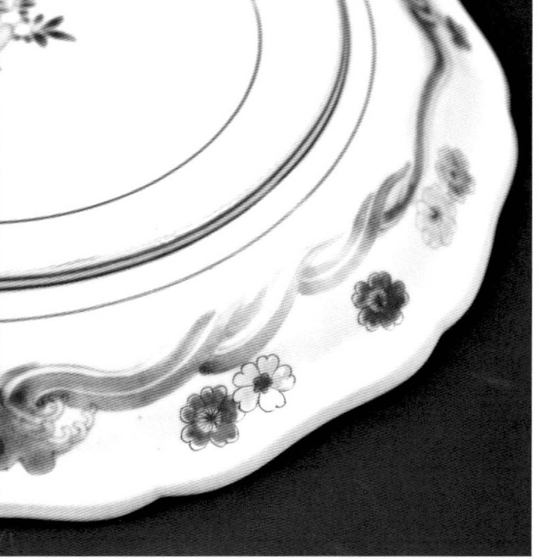

Iroe Hanamon Rinkazara, lobed dish with design of peony and stylized flower c.1690 - c.1720; Diameter 28.5cm; Private collection.

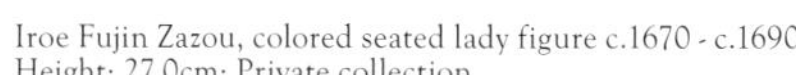

Iroe Fujin Zazou, colored seated lady figure c.1670 - c.1690 Height: 27.0cm; Private collection.

plate are drawn with a simple line rendering that gives the piece a distinctly clean overall appearance. A typical *Kakiemon* design from the *Enpo* period (1673-1681) is directly drawn on the famed *nigoshide soji* (milky white base porcelain) without any underglaze. But the outlines of the chrysanthemum, camellia and peony leaves were initially underglazed, then touched up with green and yellow colors that is more typical of the *Nabeshima* style. The way the plum is drawn on this plate is typical *Kakiemon*. Because this plate displays similarities to signed *Kakiemon* wares from the *Genroku* era (1688-1704), it is understood that it comes from the same lineage.

Although standing *Kakiemon* figurines are relatively common, sitting figurines are rare. Resting their elbows on an armrest, these figurines project a relaxing atmosphere. The shapes of the two figurines are almost identical, meaning that they were probably made from the same mold. The head, arms and body are produced separately, and then pasted together, which accounts for a slight difference in assembly. The decorative patterns on their *kimonos* are slightly different that make them look all the more like sisters.

Dish : Chirashi sushi

After preparing steamed rice lightly flavored with sushi-vinegar, the rice was mixed with cut burdock roots, carrots and lotus roots. An appropriate portion of the mixed rice was placed on the plate with toppings of kinshi-tamago (thin cut eggs), nori (seaweed laver), shrimps, broiled eel, rape blossoms, lily bulbs and Japanese pepper tree leaves to colorfully decorate the festive dish.

Sometsuke Kiku Ryusuimon Zara (under glaze blue flowing chrysanthemum design plate), c.1680 - c.1730; Diameter 19.0cm, Height 5.7cm.
Dish : Cooked eggplant and herring.

Summer delicacy with Seiki Nabeshima

Like kids in a candy store, we were thrilled by the display of the decorous *sometsuke* (underglaze blue) wares in front of us that came from the golden era of *Nabeshima*. Iketani-san and Hirose-san could not hide their excitement, even during the pre-meeting for this interview.

"In comparison, *Seiki Nabeshima—Nabeshima* ware from this golden era—may not have the vigor of an antique pot, but its refined design shines above the rest. As the most prestigious tableware in Japan, it has been the vessel for the best of Japanese cuisine," Iketani explained.

As we listened to his commentary, chef Hirose was busy working his magic in the

Sometsuke Suisen Karahanatsunagimon Zara (under glaze blue plate with daffodil foliage pattern), c.1690 - c.1720; Diameter 21.0cm, Height 4.9cm.
Dish : Fried sea eel and broad beans.

Sometsuke Goho Karahanamon Zara (under glaze blue plate with foliage pattern), c.1680 - c.1690; Diameter 20.0cm, Height 4.9cm.
Dish : Shredded ise-ebi (lobster) and gourd with seasoning.

kitchen: shredded gourd with a touch of dressing added color to the blue glazed ware, while a couple of grilled *ayu* (sweetfish) swam in the waves of *Nabeshima*.

"The *Nabeshima* wares here today had no signs of being previously used. That would mean I was the first chef to place food on these centuries' old masterpieces, so that made me a little nervous. It was a great experience to serve food with these wares since they made my dishes look more refined," said Hirose.

The *Nabeshima* wares were truly works of art.

Sometsuke Seiji Seigaihamon Zara (under glaze blue celadon plate with blue wave design), c.1680 - c.1730; Diameter 19.0cm, Height 5.0cm.
Dish : Nagara river ayu with tadezu (polygonum leaf seasoning).

The Porcelain

When *Nabeshima* wares are used as a food platter, they project a noticeably different ambience from other *Imari* wares, for they elevate the quality of the food they hold. Typically, *Nabeshima* wares have a tall base with a gradual rise from the center to the outer diameter creating depth to the porcelain. The *gosun-zara* (approx. 15cm diameter plate) and *nanasun-zara* (approx. 21cm diameter plate) of *Ko-Nabeshima* (old *Nabeshima*) that we previously introduced were early period *Nabeshima* wares with less depth, but with brilliant overglaze painting. The wares featured here are from around the *Genroku* period (1688-1704).

The *kodai* (high base) and the deep *mokuhai* (wooden cup) style is typical of the *Seiki Nabeshima*. The higher base is believed to be an effort to express formality, as were the plates with three legs at the bottom. The higher base helped the plate to stand out when served with multiple dishes on a single tray.

How does the *mikomi* (depth of the plate) affect the way a dish is served? When we asked that question to the chef, he replied that the steep curve toward the rim obviously makes it difficult to place any food around the edges, so naturally, the food was placed at the center. As a result, the raised sides of the rim surrounded the food in the center, inviting the onlooker to focus on the presented dish. Although the porcelain wares used at the middle and bottom of page 82 are not of the *mokuhai* (wooden cup) style, they both illustrate how the beautifully designed rims bring about the food in the center.

The assortment of *hachi* (bowl) and *choko* (sake cup) on page 83 all have designs on their exterior, which is different from the larger porcelain plates; however, the unique design of *Nabeshima* results in the same formal tone. The *shuki* (sake utensil) accompanying the *Nabeshima* wares is an overglazed *Kakiemon* in the shape of a *hechima* (gourd) with a handle on top. The leaf on the side is in fact a lid that you can open to pour the sake into the utensil.

Sometsuke Amihamon Zara (under glaze blue plate with weaved wave design), c.1740 - c.1820; Diameter 18.8cm, Height 5.0cm.
Dish : Sesame vinegar flavored jellyfish and cucumber beach silvertop plant style.

Sometsuke Kabudaikonmon Zara (under glaze blue plate with turnip-radish design), c.1670 - c.1680; Diameter 19.3cm, Height 4.2cm.

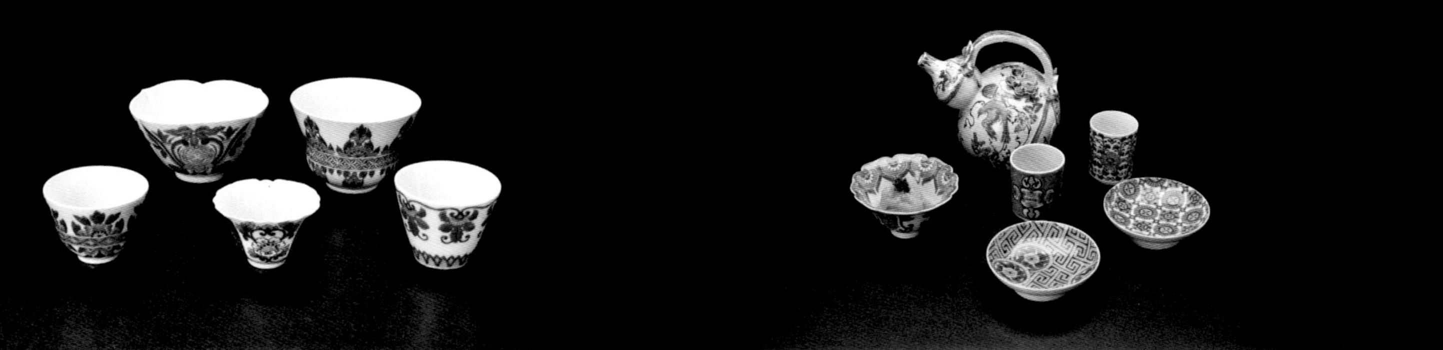

Back row from left : Sometsuke Karahanamon Rinka Bachi (under glaze blue bowl with foliage pattern); Sometsuke Karahana Shippo Tsunagimon Bachi (under glaze blue bowl with Japanese cloisonné pattern).
Front row from left : Sometsuke Karahana Shippo Tunagimon Choko (under glaze blue sake cup with Japanese cloisonné pattern); Sometsuke Karahana Rinka Choko (under glaze blue sake cup with foliage pattern); Sometsuke Kiku Karahanamon Choko (under glaze blue sake cup with chrysanthemum pattern); c.1680 - c.1720.

From left : Sometsuke Karahana Tunagimon Rinka Bachi (under glaze blue bowl with foliage pattern) with squid seasoned with sea urchin; Iroe Budo Torimon Hisagogata Saketsugi (gourd-shaped sake ewer with overglazed grapevine and birds); Sometsuke Kiku Karahana Jimonzume Choko (under glaze blue sake cup with chrysanthemum foliage pattern); Sometsuke Karahana Jimonzume Choko (under glaze blue sake cup with foliage pattern); Sometsuke Shippo Karahana Jimonzume Zara (under glaze blue plate with Japanese cloisonné foliage pattern). Front center : Sometsuke Karahana Raimon Zara (under glaze blue plate with flower and thunder pattern) Sake ewer, c.1670 - c.1700; Sake cup and bowl, c.1690 - c.1720; Plate, c.1700 - c.1740.

Sometsuke Sansuimon Ozara—blue underglaze large plate with stylized mountain and stream pattern c.1630 - c.1640; Diameter 45.0cm, Height 12.5cm. Dish : Hamo (sea eel) and matsutake mushroom shabushabu with mizuna (Japanese mustard greens) and sudachi (citrus sudachi)

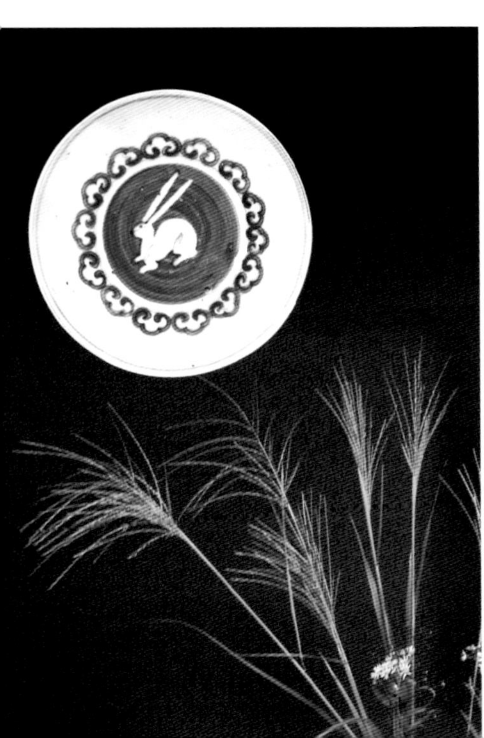

Moon-watching with Imari

Honoring the Harvest Moon has been a long tradition in Japanese culture.

"How about we go with the *Tsukimi* (moon watching) theme this time? I think a grand presentation of some seasonal harvest using a large *Shoki Imari* plate for a good *nabe* (hot pot) would look fantastic!" said Iketani-san.

Without missing a beat, Chef Hirose replied, "Then let me prepare a *hamo-matsu* dish!"

Since the start of this feature, the two men have formed a great chemistry with each other. As we sat wondering what *hamo-matsu* was, the chef was busy working his magic. Moments later, Hirose brought out the large *Shoki Imari* plate, beautifully covered with thinly cut *hamo* (sea eel) and large *matsutake* mushrooms. Accompanied by an assortment of *usagimon gosun zara*, which features a rabbit design theme and is approx. 15cm in diameter, the table was prepared for a festive feast.

The Porcelain

Large plates are typical of *Shoki Imari*. Its popularity and large-scale production, centered around the Yambeta kiln in Arita, peaked around 1630-1640. With a relatively small *kodai* (base), the underglaze process, performed before firing, attributed to the wet rich finish of the plate's design. In many of the authentication writings on the outer box, the pieces were labeled as *obachi* (large bowl) rather than *ozara* (large plate).

In the history of Japanese ceramics, large plates that exceeded diameters of 40 centimeters were not produced until the dawn

Top two plates : Sometsuke Nami Usagimon Zara—blue underglaze plate with wave and rabbit pattern c.1620 - c.1640; Diameter 14.0cm. / Bottom from left : Sometsuke Fukizumi Usagimon Zara—blue underglaze plate with sprayed ink rabbit pattern c.1630 - c.1640; Diameter 14.0cm. / Sometsuke Nami Usagimon Zara (Nabeshima)—blue underglaze plate with wave and rabbit pattern c.1690 - c.1720; Diameter 14.5cm. / Sometsuke Shironuki Usagimon Zara—blue underglaze plate with white rabbit drawing c.1630 - c.1640; Diameter 14.7cm.

Sometsuke Nami Usagimon Zara c.1620 - c.1640; Diameter 20.5cm.
Dish : Tai Matsukawazukuri
(sea bream sashima pine bark style).

Sometsuke Umekarakusamon Hyogatahei—blue underglaze gourd shaped bottle with plum vine pattern; Height 22.4cm. Sometsuke Baikamon Tsutsugata Choko—blue underglaze cylindrical sake cup with plum flower pattern both c.1610 - c.1630; Top diameter 7.3cm, Height 9.0cm.

of *Karatsu* ware. The famous *Ekaratsu Matsumon O-zara* (a *Karatsu* large plate with stylized pine pattern)—designated as an Important Cultural Property at the Umezawa Memorial Museum—has a diameter of 44.5 centimeters, which is about the same size as the *Shoki Imari* plate shown here. Large plates of this size were probably used in the *Edo* period (1603-1867) to serve *sashimi* at various gatherings.

Rabbits that grace the *nanasun-zara* (approx. 21cm-diameter plate) and the *gosun-zara*, were believed to be a symbol of fertility and rich harvest. They were one of the favorite design motifs applied to porcelain wares during the *Edo* period (1603-1867). The depiction of rabbits playing in the waves is thought to be an illustration of the lyrics from a *yokyoku* (vocal section of the music used in traditional Japanese *Noh* theater) that appears in the *Chikubushima* performance.

The *hyokei* (gourd shaped) sake ewer and the cylindrical sake cup are both designed with vertically running *shinogimon* (ridge pattern) and blue underglaze drawings on the surface, which is a style that has appeared in the early periods of *Shoki-Imari*. The cylindrical sake cups were also called *tsutsumuko* and *nozoki*, used to serve small portions of rare delicacies as well as various spices; however, today they are often used to drink sake.

SHOP INFORMATION

The Restaurant : Kaiseki Ichimonji

After devoting years of his earlier career to being a special kaiseki (traditional multi-course Japanese cuisine) chef for chaji (meals before formal tea ceremony), Chef Hirose Kazuhiko opened his own place in Kagurazaka. The restaurant is treasured as one of the few places that offers authentic Japanese cuisine, guarding the harmonic importance of ryori (cuisine), shitsurai (care to the space, occasion and atmosphere) and utsuwa (wares).

place : 3-6-46 Kagurazaka, Shinjuku-ku, Tokyo, Japan

tel : 81-(0)3-5206-8223

https://ge49400.gorp.jp/

SHIN ZEN BI

真繕美

il restauratore

A special inside report on the art of antique ceramics restoration

Antique art and artifacts that have endured the test of time for hundreds or even thousands of years can often be damaged, despite great efforts taken by the caretaker. To ensure these priceless treasures survive for generations, restoration becomes an important process, of which the responsibility rests on the current caretaker's shoulders. This report will give you a revealing look into the fascinating world of antique ceramics restoration, as we visit the workshop of Japan's most respected conservators, Mayuyama Koji and his son Yu.

The owner thought the gyokkoshun shaped (pear-shaped, Yuhuchunping) vase purchased a while back was in fairly good condition, but after bringing the vase to Mr. Mayuyama's workshop for inspection, he discovered that it had been heavily restored. With the permission of the owner, the vase was disassembled into more than 60 pieces so it could be restored properly.

We were presented with a rare opportunity to visit and see how Mayuyama Koji and his son Yu restore antique ceramics. The item they were restoring was an elaborate blue and white porcelain vase designed in the Chinese Yuan Dynasty (1271-1368).

SECTION | 001

We received a call from Mr. Mayuyama, who said, "We just received a very interesting restoration order. Would you like to come see it?"

What awaited us when we arrived at the workshop was a devastating scene (Picture Above). A porcelain vase lay in pieces. After being temporarily assembled with mending tape, we recognized that it was a beautiful gyokkoshun shaped (pear-shaped, Yuhuchunping) vase of Chinese origin with an elaborate underglaze blue design.

Koji explained: "According to the owner, it is from the Chinese Yuan Dynasty (1271-1368). At the time of purchase, the owner was told that it had been restored, and the porcelain vase looked to be in good condition. It was initially brought to us for general maintenance.

Father and son antique art restoration masters, Mayuyama Koji and his son Yu.

Pre-assembling the broken pieces into three large parts using mending tape to predetermine how the final vase should look.

As we inspected the vase, we eventually found that it has been extensively restored. With the owner's permission, we carefully dismantled the restored components and found that it was assembled from more than 60 pieces."

The owner was obviously very surprised to hear about the severity of the vase's condition. That's when Koji contacted us and said, "The restoration of this vase would be a great project for ME NO ME to follow."

He explained to us that this kind of restoration process begins from carefully disassembling the previous restoration. Then, the dismantled pieces are temporarily pre-assembled to get an image of how the final restoration should be handled. Depending on the extent of the damage, restoration assembly can be completed in one sitting, using polymer-based glue, then applying pressure to allow the glue to be absorbed. However, in this instance, they had discovered a few issues...

"First, there are some missing fragments from the neck and body of the vase, so we have to rebuild the base surface and reproduce the underglaze blue paint. The other issue is much more serious. All of the edges of the fragmented pieces had been filed down at the time of the previous restoration," said Yu.

Usually, when porcelain wares are broken due to a mishap, they can be restored relatively easy, even if they were smashed into more than 100 pieces, but with this vase, all the pieces, down to the small fragments, had been filed or sanded down. When that is done, it creates several one-tenth of a millimeter gap between the pieces when they are put together. That means each little gap must then be carefully filled to complete the restoration, which Yu explained can take a significant amount of time.

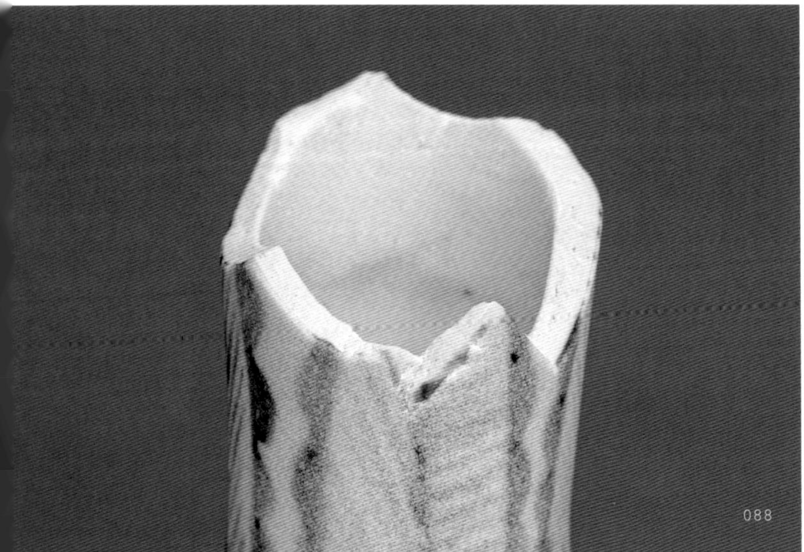

"We are assuming that this was done by the previous restorer, but I'm really confused as to why anyone would do such a thing. It's an uncommon practice anywhere in the world, and it's just not efficient," he said with a puzzled face.

In this article, we will follow the entire restoration process of this antique porcelain vase.

In the meantime, our advice to our readers is to not to discard any broken pieces of your treasure for future restorations!

SECTION | 002

When we visited the workshop about a month after our first visit, the blue and white vase was standing on its own. It seemed like a leap from the last time we saw the vase, which was covered in mending tape.

"It has been a struggle," Yu said with a wry smile. "It's standing upright on its own, but as we explained earlier, the edges of each broken piece had been filed down so it was impossible to put them all together without any gaps. Right now, I have assembled the vase with some special glue to get a better idea of how the restoration should proceed forward."

According to Yu, this pre-assemble process is important to grasp the overall image of the final product to avoid deviations from its original shape. This can easily occur if the restoration is initiated from the upper or lower part of the vase without a good understanding of how the final product should look.

"We used a special glue that easily comes apart by heat. The restoration will be done in three large sections."

As he explained, Koji took out an alcohol burner and began heating the porcelain vase (right top).

"The heat source can be anything from hot water, a hairdryer or a kotatsu (Japanese foot warmer). In this case, since the vase will completely fall apart if it's entirely heated, I am using this burner to just warm the parts where needed. This is the most convenient method."

Watching Koji heat the vase with an alcohol burner was an awkward sight indeed.

After a few minutes of rotating the vase above the burner, it was split in two different sections (right bottom).

"The process gets really detailed from here on. First, we begin filling the small gaps and cracks," Yu said as he mixed some resins and various color pigments for the restoration.

Then Koji offered this narrative: "We'll be using the same materials we used for the restoration of the Karatsu teacup in the past. However, because this time the material is porcelain, the mixing ratios will be slightly different. Also, because the outside and inside texture and colors are different on this vase, we will use different mixtures to recreate the original appearance. We will need to use different mixture ratios for the base material on the outside and inside since they look and feel very different. This time, we will start from the inside. The color is somewhat of a skin tone, brownish gray, which we will try to emulate. Since it is on the inside of the vase, we won't spend too much time matching the color, but we know from experience that some people take a peek inside and notice differences in color. I guess this attention to detail is an important commitment the Mayuyama family tries to preserve."

Overseas, we were told that some restorations are performed by wrapping a broken vase or jar to hold it together, then pouring the resin material inside. Then, after stirring the resin enough to make an inner layer, the leftover resin is poured out. A quick but not particularly impressive way of restoration.

After making the mixture, then carefully checking and adjusting its color, Yu took a moment to go over the next step in his mind. He placed a small portion of the mixed material on his finger and began applying it to the cracks inside, like a makeup artist, as he gently applied the material and filling in the cracks with his fingers.

"There are occasions when we use tools for this process, but this time I want to make sure that the cracks are fully filled. Also, there are hairline marks from the potter's wheel on this

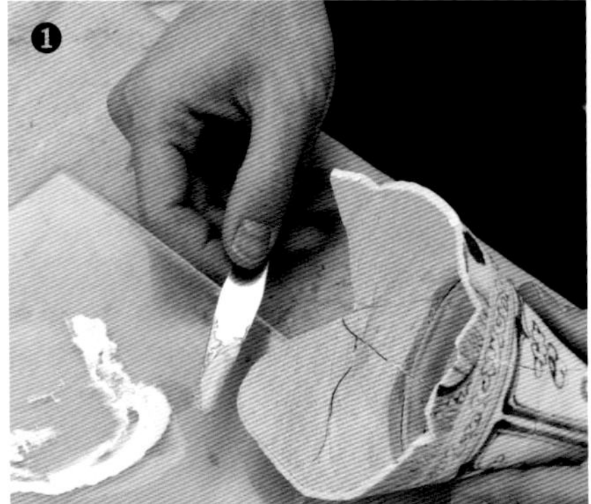

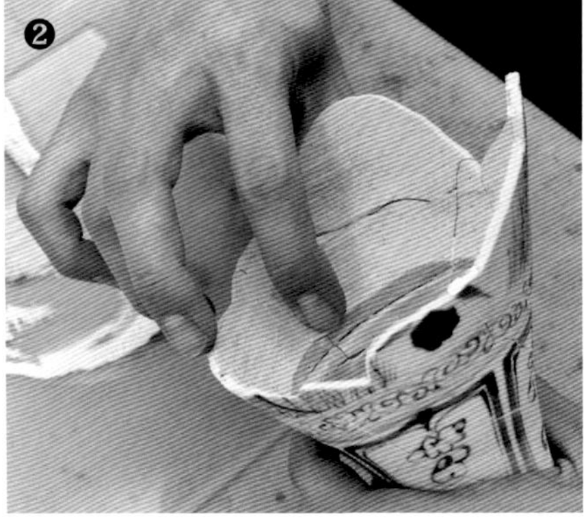

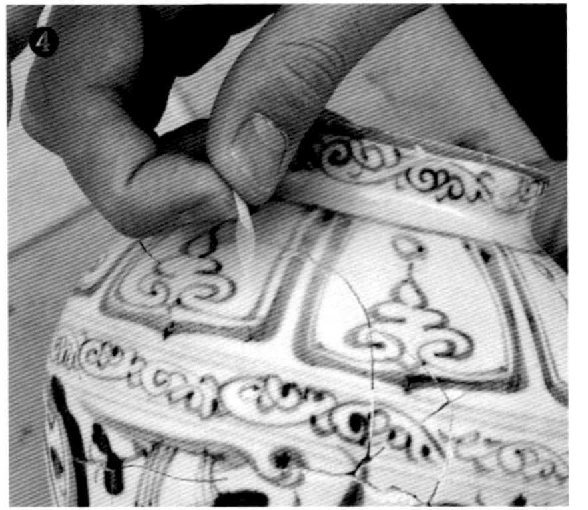

1. Mixing resin and pigments to match the original color and texture.
2. Filling in the cracks. Tools are sometimes used, but this time, the process is performed by hand to recreate the original hairline marks from the potter's wheel.
3. Even the bottom portion of the vase had complete holes.
4. When filling the holes, mending tape is applied outside to prevent excess material from bleeding out.
5. Just the right amount of resin, knowledge gained from years of experience, is applied to fill the cracks and holes.
6. After filling in cracks and holes, the matière, like the hairline of the potter's wheel, is recreated.
7. After drying, the mending tape is removed, and the excess material is scraped off.
8. Following the restoration of the inside of the vase, six more layers are applied in the restoration process.

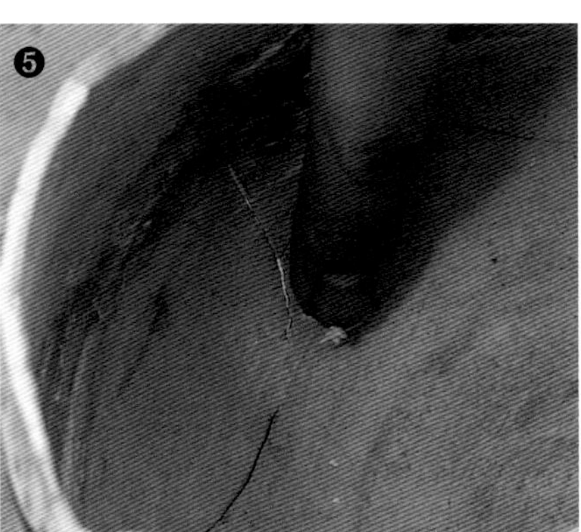

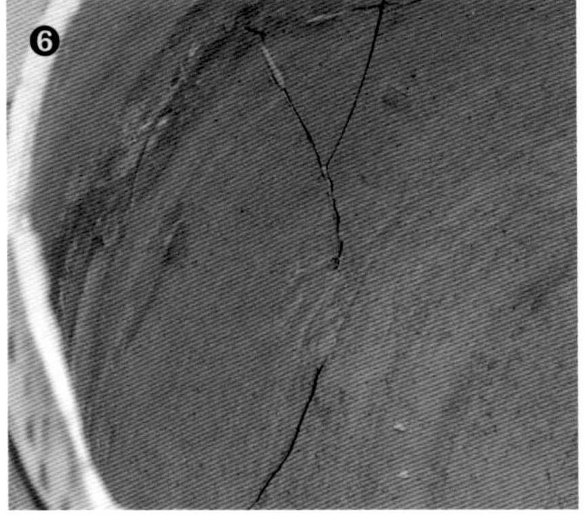

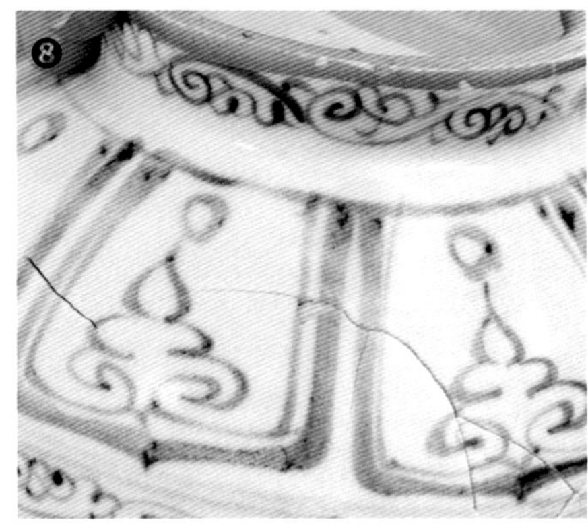

piece, so I want to make sure we don't disturb the pattern. I will recreate the marks by moving my hands sideways."

Now, that's what we call attention to detail, we told him.

"Well, we try, at least to the extent that my fingers can reach," he replied with a chuckle.

After filling all the cracks from the inside, the vase was left to dry. It was then inspected and retouched as was necessary.

"Most cracks can be processed this way, but if there are bigger gaps or holes, it is done differently. In those cases, we put the broken pieces together and tape the outside with mending tape to prevent the applied materials from bleeding out. We then fill the gaps with base material and let it dry. After drying, we scrape the excess material using knives and other tools. Even after this first process, there are about five more layers to be applied, which include the white base material, buffing material, painting, glass coating in place for the underglazing and the final finish. Therefore, this very first base material has to be done right and carefully to set up for the processes that come later."

There are meticulous steps that must be applied to the outside, so restoring the inside correctly to stabilize the restoration is very important," says Koji.

SECTION | 003

It was already around the end of summer when we received a call from Mayuyama, who told us that the base restoration was completed. When we arrived at the workshop, the porcelain vase was still split into two parts, but when we took a closer look, we noticed that the inside surface was completely restored, and the white base on the outside was also devoid of cracks and gaps. Restoring large gaps and holes is one thing but filling all the small cracks that were less than 1mm wide was surely a painstaking process.

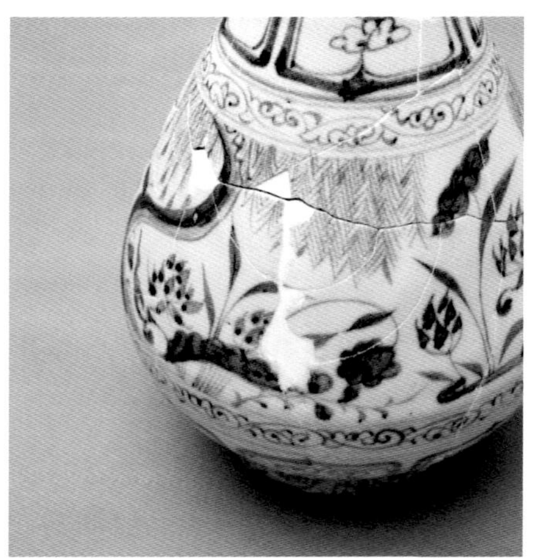

"It took a little bit more time than we expected, but we finished restoring the structural integrity of the vase so it can stand freely on its own now," Yu said, as he joined the two parts together to form a perfect fit.

The porcelain vase had now recovered its elegant gyokkoshun shape (pear-shape). Both the father and son looked unphased, but we were blown away knowing that this vase was once in more than 60 pieces and now the beautiful curved lines of the original vase had been completely restored. "From here, we will begin to recreate the top opening, which is missing a big chunk, and restore the painting on the surface," Koji explained. "To recreate that missing piece, we start by mixing the same porcelain material in powder form with resins to form the base (page 92 top right). We call this powder material suna (sand), and we have a few varieties with different particle sizes. Since this vase is underglazed, we will not be using the suna (sand) with the finest particle size. Each porcelain ware is different, and the condition of the base can be quite unique. For example, Nabeshima and Tokkayo (De-hua-yao) wares of China have a very fine base material with high transparency. For restoration of such porcelain wares, we use suna (sand) with finer

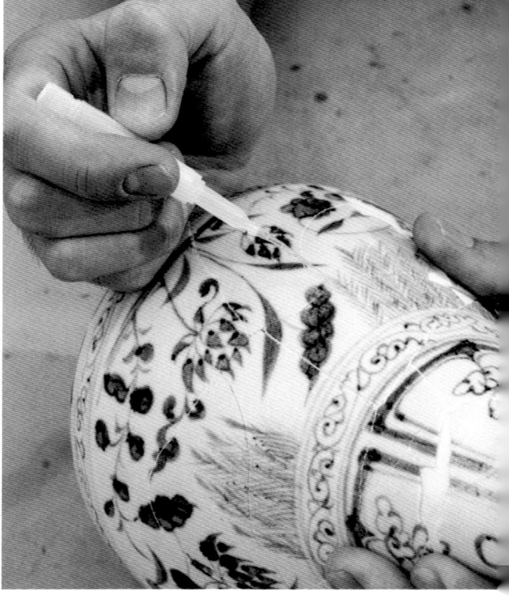

particles, but it's not as simple as selecting the finest particle size you can find and applying it. The characteristic of the base material varies depending on time periods and the original production method when it was first created. We carefully study the original material and try to come up with a unique compound suitable for the restoration project. We also preserve all the powder particles of past restoration work of antique wares for future use. Besides selecting the right material and compound, it is how we produce the mixture that define the texture and reflection of the final base. All this is knowledge that can only be acquired from experience."

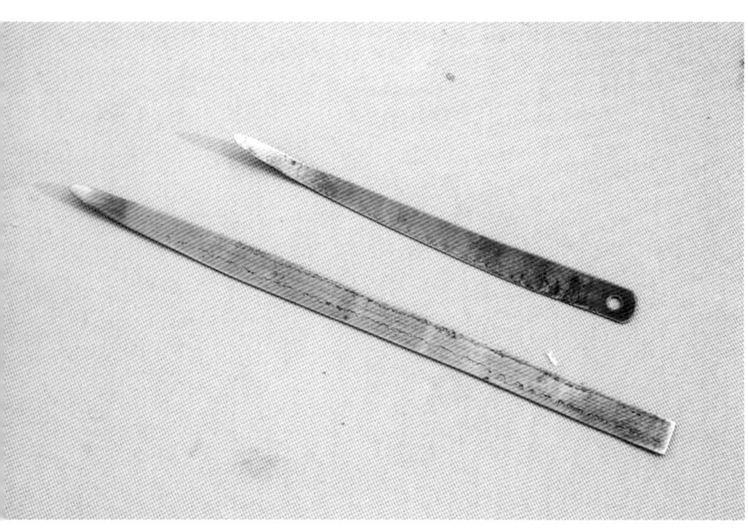

Yu's favorite spatula. A tool that he inherited from his great grandfather (top).
"This was originally a measuring spoon that my father modified into a spatula," said Yu (bottom).

The Mayuyama family uses suna, a white powder made from ground porcelain stone mixed with liquid resin.

While his father spoke, Yu was recreating the top mouth of the vase, kneading the compound then applying it with his favorite spatula.

"When the compound cures to a clay-like viscosity, I will reconstruct the shape of the top spout with my fingers," he said. "I have studied how the spout of the gyokkoshun (pear shape) should look from other examples and graphic images. The overall balance with the rest of the jar will be important, so I will carefully reconstruct the shape and angles. The process will take some time so you will probably see the result on your next visit."

The next step is restoring the underglaze, referencing the design that remains intact. Rather than describing with words, let us follow the process with pictures (page 93).

Koji explains: "The color shade of the underglaze can be quite different depending on each porcelain ware. Based on two or three shades of blue, we try to reach the desired color by adding some green, black and red. In most cases, the underglaze has a stronger black tone and less red, so we try to match the color by making samples on a few glass templates. Since it's easier to make a color darker, I usually start from lighter shades and gradually work my way up to the desired shade and intensity. With underglaze, the light and darker shades are called *dami*, which occurs from bleeding. The pigment particles in the paint are relatively coarse, so you need to paint rather quickly. The state of the base surface is also important. It is important to apply the underglaze while the surface is still a bit soft to allow the color to bleed into the surface. The depth in color can only be created by allowing it to sink into the base material. To finish the process, we use a fine needle and poke at the surface to sink in the pigment."

We were surprised that he was more than willing to share his trade secrets to us in restoring antique porcelain wares.

The amount of care and attention, the level of craftsmanship is incredible.

Applying the filling mixture to reconstruct the neck. The final sculpting will be done by hand once mixture begins to cure.

Reshaping the neck to its original form, the final form is envisioned in the restorer's mind. Balance is paramount.

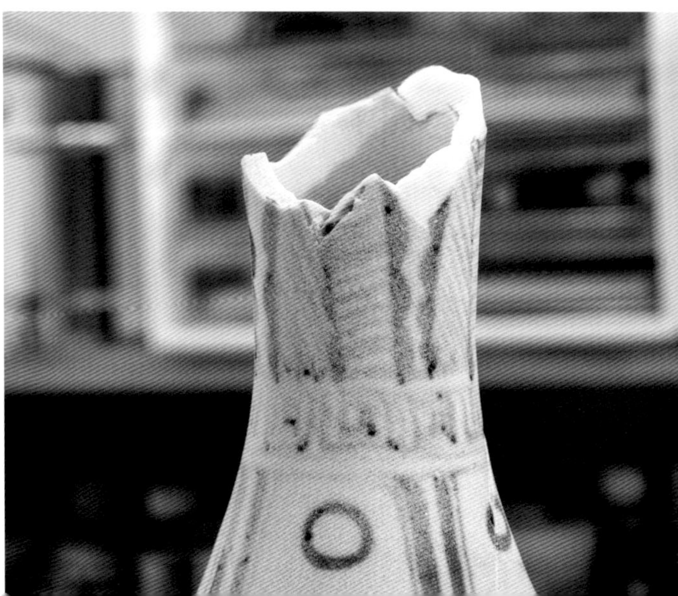

❶

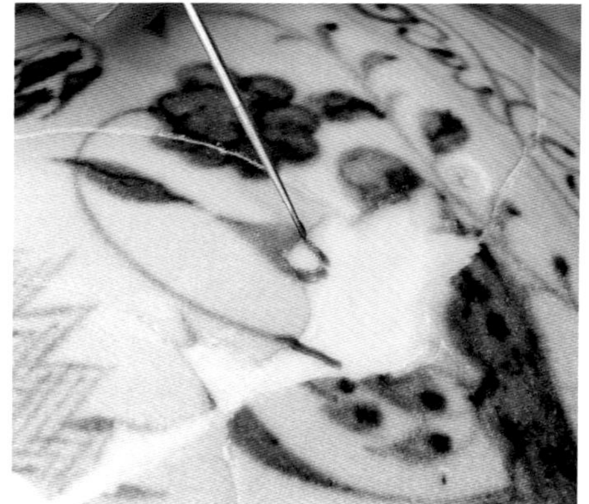
❷

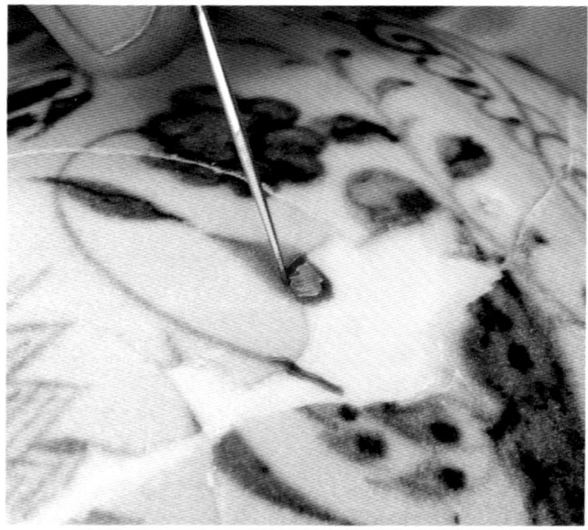
❸

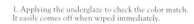

1. Applying the underglaze to check the color match. It easily comes off when wiped immediately.

2. Recreating the leaf of the peony flower. First, the contour of the leaf is drawn using a needle.

3. After the contour is drawn, the inner area is colored by applying pigment in repeated strokes.

4. Referencing the undamaged part of the vase, the leaf veins are carefully recreated, initially applying a dark shade, then poking the area to let the color settle in.

5. Like the leaf vein, the adjacent leaves are recreated drawing the contour first then filling out the inner area, referencing the images of the undamaged area.

6. Imitating the original drawing, the light and dark tones are recreated by adding a little more pigment and poking the area to adjust the shades.

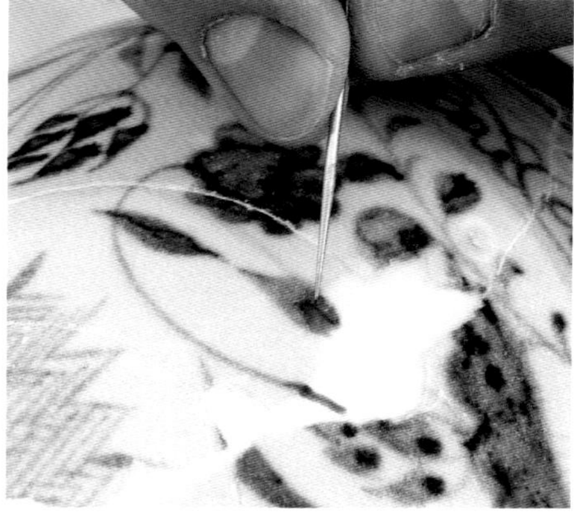
❹

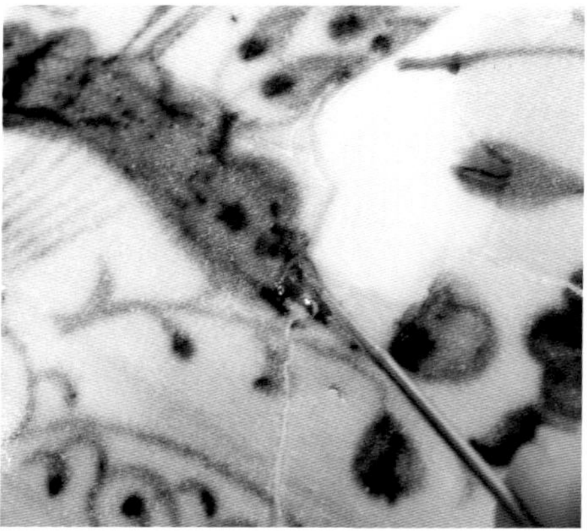
❺

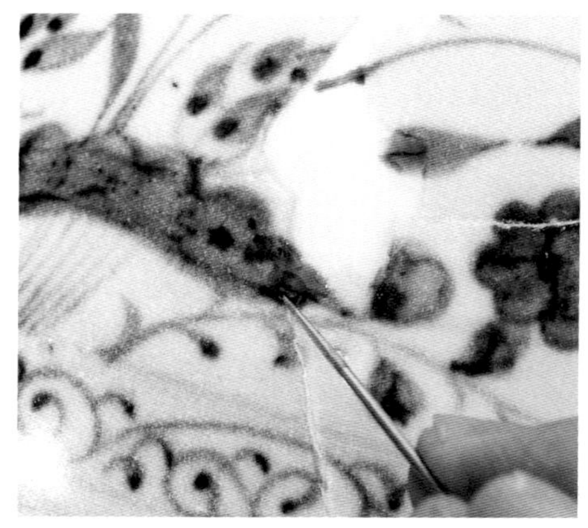
❻

On the left is the vase after the reconstruction process of the top spout. On the right is the vase with the bashoba (Japanese banana leaf) design restored. Parts below the neck were also restored with underglaze.

SECTION | 004

When we arrived at the Mayuyama workshop for our last in-depth interview, the gyokkoshun vase, despite still showing some bare white surfaces, had regained its original form. They had left half of the repaired neck unglazed to show us the repair process.

"For the next steps, we will be adding the underglaze design to the top part of the vase opening before finishing it off with the glaze coat. If you compare the parts that we are working on with the undamaged surfaces, you can see the colors appear quite differently between the glazed areas and unglazed areas," Yu commented.

The difference was indeed obvious between the bare white surface, the areas with the underglaze and the parts that were glazed in its original form. When you touch the surface, you can also tell that there is slight surface deviation.

"With most porcelain wares, the design is drawn with the underglaze, and then the entire surface is applied with glazing before putting them into the kiln. When we restore these wares, we coat the repaired area with a mixture of liquid resin and some pigments to give it a subtle blue shade, in place of the original glaze. This process helps to turn down the excessive glossiness of the newly applied material and

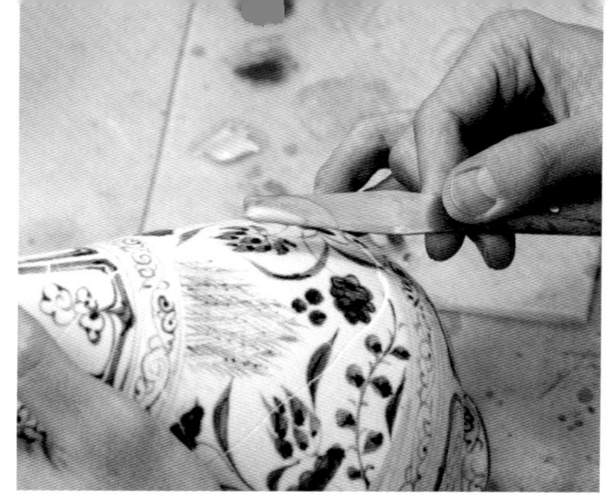

❶

1. Applying a special coating over the underglaze in place of the original glaze. Five color variations are used to lightly and thinly apply the coating. All the colors are mixed for every project to match the original tone.

2. After matching the color, the mixture is evenly spread over the underglaze with a spatula.

3. Like a master plasterer, the coating is quickly applied, eliminating the surface deviation.

4. The final process is performed by Mayuyama Koji: It is important to eliminate traces of the restored area.

5. A quick and subtle brush stroke.

6. This final step is done to bring out the underglaze beneath the surface, rather than adding more drawings.

7. Similar to the underglaze process, a fine-point needle is used to poke the surface. This process helps to make the restored surface look natural.

❷

❸

❹

❺

❻

❼

underglaze. Also, it eliminates the surface deviation to restore the original smooth surface (page 95, ① - ③)," Yu said.

As he spoke, Yu's hands were continually moving, and the porcelain vase was slowly returning to its original form in front of our very eyes. Although we knew of the process, witnessing it all happen in front of us was like watching a magic show.

It was time for the final step, which meant that it was time for Koji to take over. He spread some pigments on sketch paper and began mixing it with a very small amount of liquid resin to get a light pastel color onto his brush (page 95, ④).

"The last step is a complimentary coloring process done after glazing. What we try to do is eliminate the boundary line between the original and the newly restored area. We don't add to much color at this stage. For example, with the stem area of the peony flower, we just give it a light stroke around it to help bring out the color underneath. Then we give it a few pokes with a finely pointed needle to recreate the original texture of the underglaze. We do this to all the areas where deemed necessary and the restoration is completed," Koji said.

This final step was done in a very subtle manner, but it made a lot of difference. We were just amazed at the high level of craftsmanship of this father-and-son team. When we were shown the fully restored porcelain vase, it stood proudly in its original beauty. If we hadn't seen it with our own eyes, we wouldn't have believed that it was in pieces not that long ago.

For the next project, it would be very interesting to see this team work on an antique ware with multiple colors.

真繕美

The mystical world of spirits and demons

NETSUKE

During the Edo period of Japan (1603-1868), the cultured and the affluent carried their *Inro* (pill case) and *Tabaco-ire* (tobacco pouch) as a *Sagemono* (hanging object) attached to the *Obi* (Sash) with a *Netsuke*. As a fashion item for the fanciful Edo elites, *Netsuke* were made depicting people, animals, plants and other natural beings, as well as supernatural ones. Some of the most intriguing examples were immortal wizards and mystical beasts, which were believed to be the ultimate forms of godly creatures. The beauty of the sculpted *Netsuke* is fascinating and draws from an insatiable curiosity. Confucius once said, "Speak none of the disorderly and the supernatural." For this story, we will venture into the mystical and supernatural world of *Netsuke*.

Editorial supervisor: SAGEMONOYA

KIRIN

- Royal Hooved Creature -

Celebration of Benevolence by Mystical Beasts

The *Kirin* is the most royal of all beasts, illustrated in the *Wakan Sansai Zue* as having a deer-like body, the tail of an ox, and hooves like a horse. Its body consists of five colors, with gold around its belly. It measures about 3.6 meters in length and has round hooves and a single antler. When moving, it won't disturb even the smallest insect or plant and never travels in group. The creature appeared in the presence of a wise statesman with compassion and benevolence.

Kirin
Ivory Netsuke (18th century); Private collection.

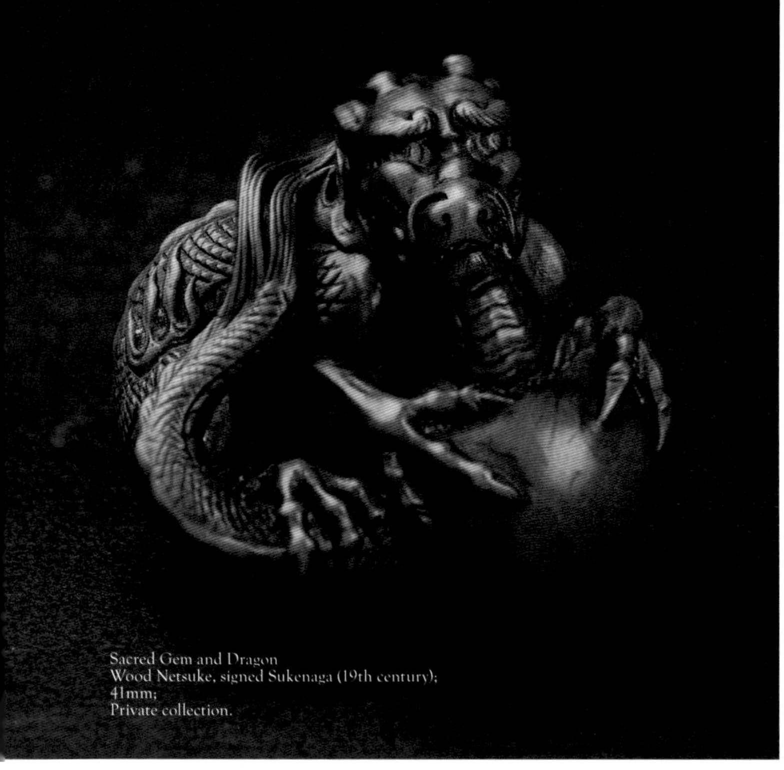

Sacred Gem and Dragon
Wood Netsuke, signed Sukenaga (19th century);
41mm;
Private collection.

Amaryu (Rain Dragon)
Ivory Netsuke, signed Kokusai
(19th century);
38mm;
Private collection.

Ryu (Dragon)
Wood Netsuke, signed Tametaka
(19th century);
39mm;
Sagemonoya.

RYU - Dragon -

The auspicious beast that roamed the heavens and blessed us with rain

The Dragon, which is a well-known mythical creature in Japan, began to appear in Chinese literature even before the common era. According to the *Wakan Sansai Zue*, "The Dragon resembles nine creatures. It possesses the head of a camel, the antlers of a deer, the eyes of an ogre, the ears of an ox, the nape of a snake, the belly of a *Shen* (monster clam), the scales of a carp, the claws of a hawk and the paws of a tiger. The Dragon blew out vapor from its mouth, which changed to clouds, rain, and even fire." This description is relevant for explaining the Dragon's strong association with water and fire.

Hiryu (Flying Dragon)
Deer antler Netsuke, unsigned
(19th century);
47mm;
Private collection.

Ryu (Dragon)

Left: Wood Netsuke, unsigned (18th century);
62mm; Private collection.

Right: Ivory Netsuke, signed Tomotada (18th century);
53mm; Sagemonoya.

NETSUKE

Appreciating the palm sized amulet

Yoshida Yukari

Director of SAGEMONOYA, the only gallery in Japan that specializes in antique Netsuke and Sagemono. An expert and researcher of Netsuke, speaking at various events worldwide. Author of numerous columns and articles in art magazines and books. Member of the International Netsuke Society. Board member of the Nihon Netsuke Kenkyukai.

Netsuke as part of the formal attire of the Samurai

The subjects of *Netsuke* are all things in the universe; however, in this instance, we want to focus mainly on the imaginary beings that fascinate many of the collectors in the west. The immortal wizards and creatures are often depicted in a unique way, which sometimes reminds us of the lost perspectives of modern people, the ability to imagine things that we have never seen. For this special feature, we asked the owner of the only gallery in Japan that specializes in antique *Netsuke*, Yoshida Yukari of Sagemonoya, to walk us through the fascinating world of *Netsuke*.

For starters, we must ask the question: what is the subject or creature most commonly depicted in *Netsuke*?

Yoshida: "Well, that is very difficult to say. Since *Netsuke* has been a fashion accessory at different times and in different regions, it is hard to pick out what is most popular. People used to carry *Netsuke*, not only because one was their favorite, but they also considered the occasion."

I see. Time, place and occasion were of importance.

Yoshida: "Yes, exactly. For example, if it was a formal gathering of high level *Samurai*, *Netsuke* depicting the characters from ancient Chinese proverbs such as *Zhang Liang* (strategist) and *Huang Shigong* (old man) or *Guan Yu* (legendary general) were selected. A wise ruler or a heroic warrior that appears in such ancient Chinese history books and writings of Confucianism were popular motifs of *Netsuke*. A *Samurai's* formal attire included an *Inro*, as a way of showing respect to the person he was going to meet. In combination with an *Inro*, a *Netsuke* depicting a story of a legendary character was carried as an accessory."

So the *Netsuke* had a social and ceremonious meaning.

Yoshida: "Yes, also *Netsuke* with themes from *Genji Monogatari* and *Ise Monogatari* are popular as well. Such romantic stories may not seem to match the warrior image of the *Samurai*, but the Edo period was a time of peace, so there was a trend to express one's culture and intelligence by carrying items with elegant and graceful themes."

That trend must have been limited to high ranking *Samurai* families with a certain amount of wealth.

Yoshida: "Exactly. High-ranking *Samurais* only carried *Netsuke* in the early Edo period. After tobacco became widely popular, *Netsuke* accompanied tobacco cases by common folks who admired the accessory items carried by the *Samurai*. With that trend, people carried *Netsuke* depicting their family origin or the local regions. By the end of the Edo period, the motifs became much dressier, taking on all kinds of themes that were eye-catching and sometimes even humorous to attract attention."

Auspicious and holy beasts in Netsuke art

So what were some of the popular imaginary beings depicted in *Netsuke*?

Yoshida: "There were many, but the *Kirin* (page 99) probably carved by Tomotada, a famous *Netsuke-shi* (Netsuke artist) from Kyoto, is considered a masterpiece for its size and craftsmanship. In Chinese mythology, the *Kirin* is the most mystical of all beasts. It is a divine creature that only appears in the presence of wise politicians who show compassion and benevolence. Many people might recall the enthronement of the Japanese emperor on October 22 last year. The *Kirin* and the phoenix were masterly painted underneath the columns and railing of the *Takamikura* (imperial throne)."

Where did the image of the *Kirin* originate?

Yoshida: "The image of the holy beast was often depicted as a combination of living animals. As stories of the *Kirin* were told for generations, its appearance became established. The *Kirin* is mentioned in ancient Chinese literature before the birth of Christ, but its image first appears around the Donghan period (22–220 AD) in

SHISHI - Lion -

The mystical beast that crushes and eradicates evil

The *Shishi* is described in the *Wakan Sansai Zue* as the king of all beasts. They often appear sculpted on Japanese shrines and temples as guardians from evil. The *Shishi* is, without a doubt, the most popular subject of *Netsuke*. They are also believed to be very affectionate; thus, they are often sculpted as a family or as a pair showing affection to each other.

Three Shishi (Three Lions)
Wood Netsuke, signed Masayoshi (19th century);
46mm;
Private collection.

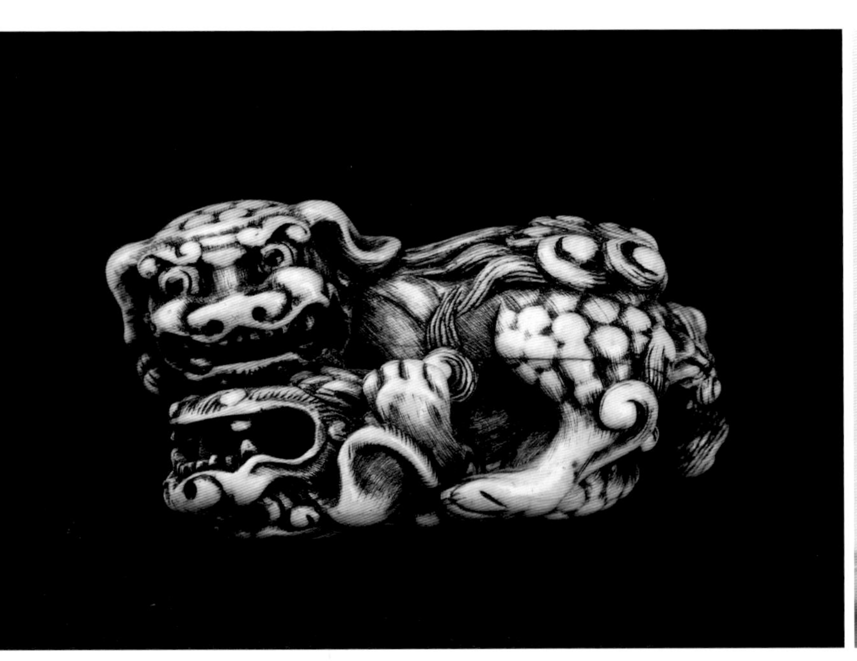

Two Shishi (Twin Lions)
Ivory Netsuke, unsigned (18th century);
53mm;
Private collection.

Shishi with peony
Wood Netsuke, signed Tametaka (18th century);
45mm;
Private collection.

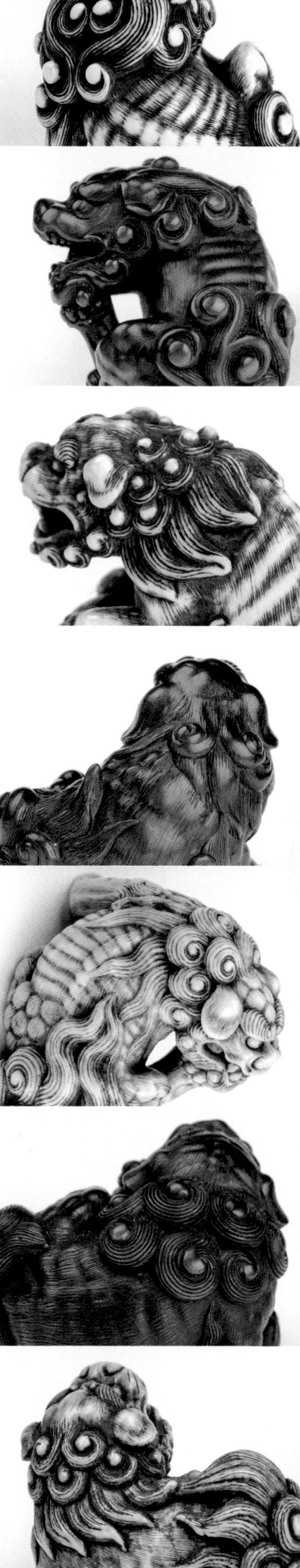

the *Setsumon Kaiji* (ancient Chinese dictionary). It also appears in the *Sansai Zue*, an encyclopedia from the Ming dynasty, which is said to be the reference for the *Kirin* depicted in the *Wakan Sansai Zue*, an encyclopedia published in Japan in 1712. The motifs of the *Netsuke* were often from such imported literature or illustrations as well as images that appear on the walls and paintings of shrines, temples and *Byobu* paintings (folding screens). The *Kirin* often resembles a deer or a horse with its body covered in scales, accompanied by rings of fire and clouds. It is a symbolic reminder that it was a holy beast. It is said that the *Kirin* is a gentle creature that never steps on a living plant or an insect, which is illustrated from its solid-hoofed legs. Most *Netsuke* and other artifacts depict the creature like a unicorn, but some versions have two horns or antlers, which suggests there is some freedom in interpretation."

Shishi (Lion) the most popular

Kirin Netsukes are said to be rare. What is the most common type of Netsuke?

Yoshida: "As far as numbers go, *Shishi* is the most common *Netsuke*."

Why is that?

Yoshida: "There are many reasons. One is its versatility. As I have mentioned before, *Netsuke* are a luxury item, so not too many people can afford to possess one for every occasion. With

An assortment of shishi netsuke. The curled mane (shishi-ge) sculpted from head to tail was where each sculptor showed off his skills.

A collection of *Shishi Netsuke* all signed Shigemasa; Private collection.

Seal Netsuke
Shishi—Ivory, signed Kokusai (19th Century);
36mm; right: engraved seal
Private collection.

Seal Netsuke
Shishi—Ivory, signed Hakusai (19th Century);
34mm;
Private collection.

Two Shishi Netsuke (19th Century);
Left : Ivory Netsuke, signed Ren(sai); 36mm;
Right : Ivory Netsuke, 42mm;
Sagemonoya.

Shishi with Ball
Ivory Netsuke (18th Century);
54mm;
Sagemonoya.

Shishi
Lacquered wood Netsuke, unsigned (17th~18th Century);
46mm;
Private collection.

these restrictions, owning a *Shishi Netsuke* is a wise choice. A *Shishi Netsuke* can be carried under most circumstances. They were acceptable to all classes of people, no matter who you were to be meeting."

So it's a safe choice?

Yoshida: "That makes it sound like it has less value, but the case is quite the opposite. The *Shishi Netsuke* is a popular choice because it wards off evil. The Japanese people, as a culture, used amulets to ward off evil. From their clothing to the furniture and tools around the house, they were superstitious and marked their belongings with auspicious symbols. *Netsuke* has also been deeply connected to the *Samurai's Katana* (sword). The *Shishi* is often depicted on the *Menuki* (sword hilt), *Tsuba* (sword guard) and other ornamental parts of the *Katana*. The *Shishi* was designed and sculpted by the likes of Goto-ke (famous sword-maker family) as well as the town's goldsmith. When creating a *Shishi*, the artists focused and competed on the design of the *Shishi-ge* (mane of lion), which is unique to the *Shishi* (page 103). The curled mane was usually sculpted from head to tail. The way the mane curled—its complexity, three dimensional design and originality—was where the sculptor

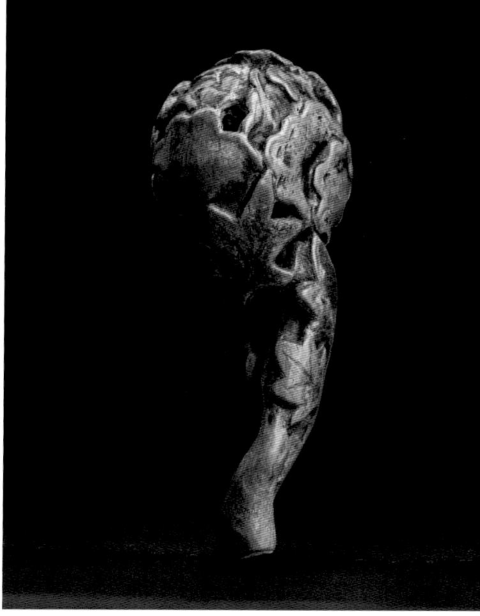

Shishi and Peony
Colored wood Netsuke (18th Century);
79mm; Private collection.

The Shishi is said to be the king of all beasts, while the peony is the master of all flowers. This Netsuke depicts a Shishi hiding inside a peony. The Shishi is designed to move inside the peony.

Left: Shishi emerging from an Egg
Ivory Netsuke, unsigned (early 19th Century);
27mm;
Sagemonoya.

Right: Shishi emerging from an Egg
Wood Netsuke, signed Raku (19th Century);
40mm;
Sagemonoya.

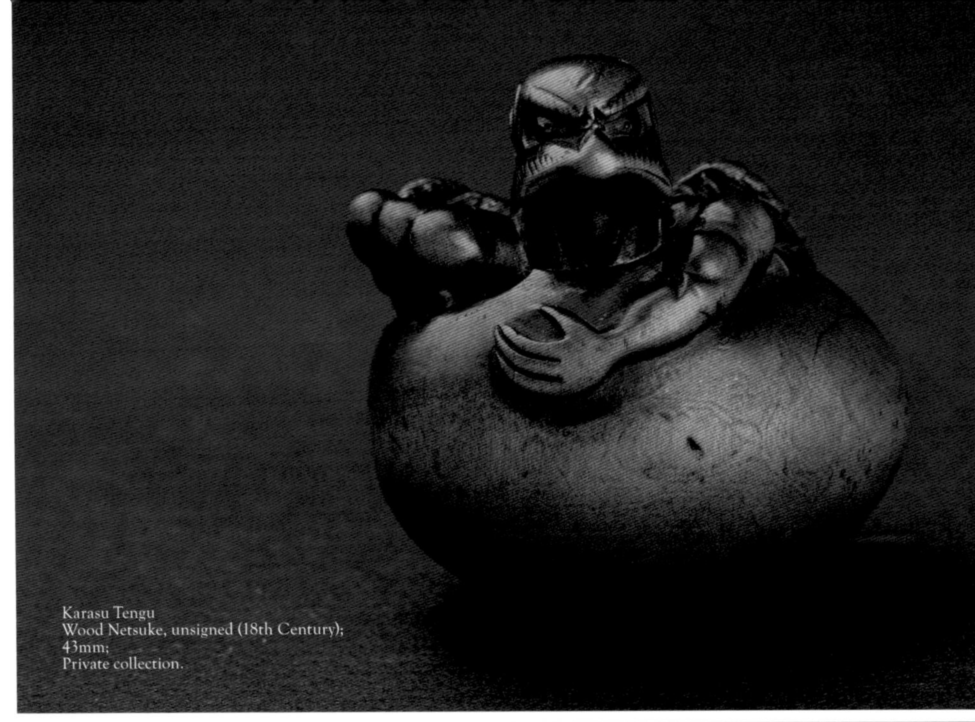

Karasu Tengu
Wood Netsuke, unsigned (18th Century);
43mm;
Private collection.

TENGU

The Beloved Mountain Apparition of Japan

The *Tengu's* myth in Japan describes an entity with wings, a bird-like beak, a red-colored face with a long nose, and dressed like a Buddhist mountain priest. In the *Wakan Sansai Zue*, the *Tengu* is categorized as a bird that can change into a human to carry out mystical deeds. As shown in the picture, the *Tengu* is born from an egg, which explains its relationship with birds. The fascination and affection for the *Tengu* as a character grew in Japan over time.

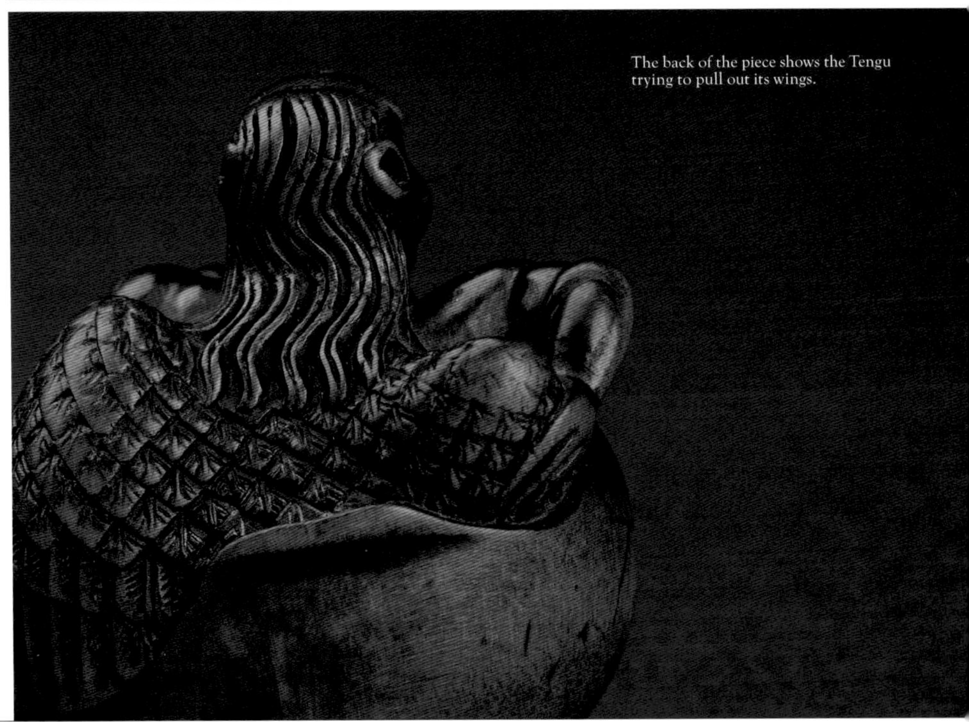

The back of the piece shows the Tengu trying to pull out its wings.

showed off his skill. The *Shishi's* bulging muscles and how the entire body was expressed are unique to each piece, so there are many elements to look for in *Shishi Netsuke*. Many of the master craftsmen in Kyoto, Osaka and all of Japan have created masterpieces of the *Shishi Netsuke* that survive today."

There seems to be various versions of the *Shishi Netsuke*.

Yoshida: "Yes, since the *Shishi* was such a popular theme, they came in various shapes and forms. Some of them have a specific meaning. For example, the *Oyako Shishi* (parent and child lion) symbolizes family prosperity. Although there is a proverb that says a lion pushes its weak cub off a cliff, the animal was actually very family-oriented and affectionate. The *Tama* (ball) of the *Tama Shishi* symbolizes wealth and prosperity; hence, it is often translated as a symbol of a prosperous business. The *Shishi-ku* depicting a lion roaring is said to ward off evil, a connotation derived from Buddha's preaching. The *Inshō Netsuke* (seal *Netsuke*), with a sculpted *Shishi*, appeared from around the 17th Century. It is believed that stamping a document or contract with such a seal prevents future misfortune."

There is a *Netsuke* with a *Shishi* coming out of an egg. (page 105 bottom)

Yoshida: "That egg is called a *Shu-jyu*. It is said that while a male and female lion were playing, their fur got tangled up and turned them into a pearl ball. According to the ancient Chinese fable, lion cubs came out from the pearl. Since then, the *Shu-jyu* has symbolized matrimonial harmony and family prosperity. However, one of the *Netsuke* I have shown today depicted two lions hugging each

HAKUZOSU

A fox disguised as a monk

Hakuzosu was a fox disguised as a monk. According to the legend, the myth of *Hakuzosu* originated in Osaka. It became widely known when it was adopted as a *Kyogen* play called *Tsurigitsune* (Fox Trapping). It is portrayed as an old white fox and often depicted wearing a monk's robe.

Hakuzosu
Ivory Netsuke, unsigned (18th Century);
61mm;
Private collection.

other. Perhaps that *Netsuke* wanted to illustrate the male and female lions before they turned into a pearl ball."

I really thought it was an egg.

Yoshida: "Actually, the *Tengu*, commonly known in Japan, is born from an egg. *Tengu* was originally the name of a shooting star in ancient China. When the name made its way to Japan, it was somehow connected to mystical mountain spirits, then given a bird-like image. Some time in history, it merged with stories of monks training in the deep mountains, and the current image of a bird-like *Tengu* was born."

We thought *Tengu* were closer to a guardian of the gods rather than a ghostly creature, but the actual characterization seems much more complicated.

Yoshida: "Yes, that's why its image is hard to grasp. But because of its kin to birds, the image often includes a bird-like beak and the belief that it was born from an egg. In the *Soken Kisho*, the first directory for *Netsuke* artists published in Japan, the *Tengu* is illustrated in relation to *Sottaku*."

What is *sottaku*?

Yoshida: "The act of poking the eggshell from the inside by a chick that is about to hatch is called '*Sotsu*'. At the same time, the poking done from the outside of the eggshell by the parent bird is called '*Taku*'. The hatching occurs when those two separate actions are simultaneous. The proverb *Sottaku-no-ki* is an expression used when two parties or actions engage in harmony. It is considered a good omen."

Some pieces are difficult to tell whether they are *Kirin* or *Shishi*.

Yoshida: "That is a *Komainu*, a guardian dog (page 108 bottom). This is a *Baku* (page 107 bottom). Since the Heian period (794–1185), *Komainu* were often paired with the *Shishi* and offered to shrines. Most *Komainu* are unicorns, but their mouths are closed. Since this one has an open mouth, it might be some other creature. The *Baku* is believed to eat up bad dreams, so it has been used as an amulet since the Muromachi period (1136–1573), and its image became widely known during the Edo period (1603–1867)."

BAKU

Expels evil and digests bad dreams

The myth of this creature dates back to ancient China; however, its depiction varies depending on the literature. In the *Honzo Komoku* (an ancient encyclopedia), the *Baku* is described as having the nose of an elephant, the eyes of a rhinoceros, the tail of an ox and the legs of a tiger. In China, the *Baku* was said to ward off evil, and its ability to eat bad dreams seems to have originated in Japan.

Baku
Ivory Netsuke, unsigned (18th century);
36mm;
Private collection.

Ho-o (Phoenix)
Wood Netsuke, signed Toyokazu (19th century); 47mm;
Sagemonoya.

From Left : Wood Netsuke, unsigned (18th Century); 45mm.
Yo (Leopard) - Wood Netsuke, unsigned (18th Century); 42mm.
Suisei (Water rhino) - Wood Netsuke, unsigned (late 18th Century); 38mm;
Sagemonoya.

KOMAINU

A sacred beast with a single horn

The *Komainu* has been around since the Heian period (794–1185) and is often placed together with the *Shishi* in shrines and temples. Widely known in Japan, this spiritual animal was the subject of very old *Netsuke*.

Komainu
Ivory Netsuke, unsigned (early 18th Century); 54mm;
Sagemonoya.

The Dragon as the master of water and a guardian from fire

Is the Dragon the most popular next to the *Shishi* when it comes to *Netsuke*?

Yoshida: "Yes, dragon *Netsuke* were quite popular. However, since they were difficult to make, their numbers in the market are relatively low. Along with the *Kirin*, the Dragon was introduced in China many years before Christ. From the Kan dynasty and onwards, the Dragon was considered as the symbol of the emperor and one of the Four Gods/Four Guardians. Also, the *Ryujin* (Dragon god) has been worshipped in many shrines and regions throughout Japan. Edo, the old name of Tokyo, used to be known for its frequent street fights and fire. Fire prevention was a serious concern for the people of Edo. The uniforms of the *Hikeshi* (firefighters) were often illustrated with the Dragon as a symbol of fire prevention. Since tobacco had an obvious association with fire, tobacco cases were often paired with a dragon *Netsuke* to ward off any unintended fire accidents. Although this might be off-topic, when the *Hokuetsu Seppu* (a book about life in the snow regions of Japan) was published in the late Edo period, it included illustrations of snowflakes. That triggered a boom in Japan to apply *Yukiwa* (snowflake) patterns on all kinds of items, including *Hai-otoshi* (ashtray) *Netsuke*, smoke pipes, tobacco cases and even on the uniforms of firefighters."

There are so many variations to the Dragon *Netsuke* you have shown us today (page 100).

Yoshida: "The images of the Dragon are unique *Netsuke* carvings. The rings of fire and clouds illustrate the godly character of the Dragon, just like the *Kirin*. However, the *Hiryu* (Flying Dragon), *Unryu* (cloud climbing dragon) and the *Amaryu* (rain dragon) themes allow for a variety of imaginative expressions original to each artist.

The Dragon made by Sukenaga (page 100 top left) is a one-of-a-kind piece. The elegant and graceful *Amaryu* (page 100 top-right) is a popular theme; the *Karakane* (bronze) *Netsuke* made by 18th-century artist Karamonoya Kyubei are among the most famous. The *Amaryu* theme was popular and lasted for a long time, with masters like Kokusai and Hakusai from the Meiji period using also the theme. Like the *Shishi*, many artists took the challenge to showcase their skills with the *Amaryu*. I think the theme encouraged bold designs from various artists because it was an imaginative creature."

GENBU - Reiki -

Symbol of Longevity and Vitality

The turtle has been a symbol of longevity since the beginning of time. When *Gogyo-setsu* (Chinese philosophy) became popular in ancient China, it was said that the turtle copulated with the snake to become the God of the North, one of the Four Orientation Gods. Because the turtle was said to live for more than a thousand years, it was believed to have obtained spiritual powers. The *Minogame* depicted with seaweed growing on the back of its shell also became one of the Four Auspicious Beasts.

Genbu
Wood Netsuke, signed Ichiraku (19th century);
Private collection.

Minogame on an Abalone
Wood Netsuke, unsigned (18th Century);
42mm;
Sagemonoya.

Minogame
Ivory Netsuke, unsigned (18th Century); 102mm; Private collection.

There was also an example of *Ho-o*, a phoenix (page 108 top left). Was it considered as one of the Four Gods?

Yoshida: "In general, the Four Gods are said to be *Seiryu* (blue Dragon), *Suzaku* (vermillion bird), *Byakko* (white tiger) and *Genbu* (black tortoise). That said, in *Enanji* (ancient Chinese literature), the *Oryu* (Dragon), *Kirin*, *Ho-o* and *Reiki* (ghostly turtle) are designated as the Four Holy Beasts and often considered equal to the Four Gods. In *Netsuke*, there really isn't a definitive distinction between the two groups. For today's interview, I borrowed two examples of *Genbu* (snake coiled around a turtle) and *Reiki* (Minogame) *Netsuke* from a private collector (page 109)."

They are all so unique in shape and form. Looking at the examples in front of us, there is definitely a distinction between *Genbu* and *Reiki*.

Yoshida: "The turtle is a symbol of longevity, and the snake symbolises vitality. So, both *Genbu* and *Reiki* represent longevity and prosperity. Compared to the Dragon, all the other *Netsuke* like the *Suzaku*, *Byakko* and *Genbu* are scarce in number."

Does that mean that having the Four Gods as a set wasn't all that important?

Yoshida: "No, it wasn't perceived as that important; otherwise, there would have been more specimens of the other three holy creatures. In fact, there is an abundance of dragon *Netsuke*, but combinations of *Suzaku* & *Ho-o* and *Genbu* & *Reiki* are much less common. There are quite a lot of *Netsuke* depicting real

SHOJO

Red-haired mountain hermit who brings good luck

In ancient Chinese literature, the *Shojo* is described as an apelike creature living in the mountains of *Yunnan* (China) and Vietnam. It is assumed that it was modeled off of an orangutan. In Japan, the *Shojo* is believed to bring good fortune and has become popular in *Noh* (Classical Japanese dance- drama).

Shojo
Ivory Netsuke, signed by Otoman (19th Century);
44mm;
Sagemonoya.

tigers but not many examples of the *Byakko*, the holy beast. It's fairly safe to say that, in the world of *Netsuke*, producing or having them as a set was not that important."

Immortal and Imaginary beings

Lastly, let's look at some immortals and imaginary beings. When one looks at books of *Netsuke*, imaginary beings with long arms (*Tenaga*) and long legs (*Ashinaga*) often appear in pictures. Were they a popular theme in the Edo period?

Yoshida: "No, not at all. They are often mentioned because of their rarity. There are a few theories about that, but, in *Netsuke*, a story originating mainly in Kyushu is said to be the origin. It was said that, in the southern seas, there was a nation of long-armed and long-legged people who cooperated when they went out to sea to fish. The long-legged person would piggyback the long-arm person, who used his long arms to catch fish. It was a theme expressing peace, and that's what the *Netsuke* in the picture (page 111 top) is depicting."

That explains the smiling expressions on these *Netsuke*. What about the one with an older man with a horse on his back?

Yoshida: "That is an immortal hermit called *Chokaro* (Chinese name Zhang Guo Lao) (page 110 bottom). He is a very famous hermit in China, one of the legendary Eight Immortals from the Chinese mythology. He is said to get around on a horse, which he can let appear and disappear at will from his gourd. The *Netsuke* is depicting such a scene."

CHOKARO

One of the favorite Eight Immortals

Chokaro is a famous hermit in China who traveled with a horse that he could make appear and disappear at will. Together with *Shoriken*, *Kanshoshi*, *Ritekkai*, *Sokokkyu*, *Ryodohin*, *Ransaika*, *Kasenko*, they form the *Hassen* group of Eight Immortals, a group similar to the Japanese *Shichifukujin* (Seven Lucky Gods).

Chokaro
Ivory Netsuke, signed Yoshitomo (18th Century);
45mm;
Sagemonoya.

TENAGA · ASHINAGA

Mild-mannered outlanders

Left : Ashinaga
Wood Netsuke, unsigned (early 18th Century);
152mm;
Sagemonoya.

Right : Tenaga-Ashinaga
Ivory Netsuke, signed Homin (19th Century);
130mm;
Sagemonoya.

GAMA SENNIN · SHISHI SENNIN

Hermits with animals

Left : Shishi Sennin
Ivory Netsuke, unsigned (18th century);
100mm;
Sagemonoya.

Right : Gama Sennin
Ivory Netsuke, unsigned (18th Century);
98mm;
Sagemonoya.

RAIDEN

- God of Lightning -

Personification of lightning

Although this *Netsuke* resembles an *Oni*, it appears to be carrying drums on its back; hence, it is presumed to be *Raiden* (or *Raijin*). The difference in appearance between the *Fujin* (god of wind) and *Raijin* (god of lightning) depicted here by *Sotatsu* (Japanese painter) is intriguing and noteworthy.

ONI - Demon -

A demon that wards off evil

The written Japanese word for *Oni* (demon) is read *Ki* in Chinese. In China, *Ki* was the word used to describe the spirits of the dead. When the word was introduced to Japan, it became associated with man-eating ogres that brought about havoc. The *Shuten-doji* and *Ibaraki-doji* that appear in narratives from the Heian period (794–1185) are examples of such ogres. With time, they began to be depicted with one or two horns on their heads and wearing tiger skin *Fundoshi* (traditional Japanese undergarment). Interestingly, the Oni is sometimes revered as a *Kishin* (ogre god) that wards off evil.

Raiden
Wood Netsuke, signed Tanri (18th century);
36mm;
Sagemonoya.

Oni
Ivory Netsuke, unsigned (18th Century);
38 mm;
Sagemonoya.

Left : Oni (with Okame on the reverse)
Ivory Netsuke, unsigned (late 18th Century);
35mm;
Sagemonoya.

Right : Oni
Wood Netsuke, unsigned (19th century);
47mm;
Sagemonoya.

I see, you can appreciate a *Netsuke* even more when you know the backstory. Then, is this the *Gama-sennin* (Chinese name Liu Hai) (page 111 bottom right)?

Yoshida: "Yes, it is, and the one next to it is the *Shishi-sennin*."

We know the *Gama-sennin*, but we've never heard of the *Shishi-sennin*.

Yoshida: "The *Gama-sennin* is not a major character, but in Japan, he is a popular subject along with the *Tekkai-sennin* (Chinese name Li Tieguai). However, not a lot is known about the *Shishi-sennin*. There is an immortal called the *Ryu-sennin*, who holds a dragon, and the *Shishi-sennin* might be a variation of such immortal. There might be other stories and folklores that have been lost in modern times."

When one looks at all these fine *Netsuke*, it seems that *Netsuke* artists weren't just skilled sculptors but true artists.

Yoshida: "Yes, and it's also a misperception if you thought *Netsuke* were originally purchased from a store shelf. *Netsuke* were usually made to order. A clan with relative power had an artisan on payroll, who took orders from the clan's members to custom-make their *Netsuke*. In towns, there were high-end haberdasheries, *Karaki* (exotic wood) wholesalers and special craft stores for ivory to make custom *Netsuke*. Most of the material used for *Netsuke* were of the highest quality. Sometimes, if a *Ranma* (transom screen) carver received an order for a screen and had leftover wood of high quality, they would carve a *Netsuke* for the client. Technically, there wasn't a profession that specialized in *Netsuke* carving. It was a painter, metal artisan, Buddha statue carver, lathe artisan, denture craftsman and other artisans working in the *Osaikudokoro* (workshop) of the clan who took orders. He used the materials and skills associated with each of their trades to make *Netsuke*. The examples of *Netsuke* that I was able to show today have all been handmade with passion and dedication by each of their creators. I am certain that the fascination and appreciation for these masterpieces will be passed on to future generations. Just to be clear, I had used the word *Netsuke* artisans for this article, but there is room for debate as to the correct way to call the creators of *Netsuke*, whether that be craftsman, artisan, artist, creator or another term."

Thank you very much for your insight.

Ryugu Castle
Ivory Netsuke, signed Kagetoshi (19th Century);
40mm;
Sagemonoya.

Gem-shaped Netsuke with a dragon coiling on the crest of a wave, elaborately designed with a hidden Ryugu Castle inside.

夢工房
YUMEKOUBOU
236 Nakano-cho, Shinmonzen-tori Yamato-oji higashiiru,
Higashiyama-ku, Kyoto-shi, Kyoto, 605-0082, Japan
Open - am11:00 - pm5:00
Closed - Tuesdays
Tel : +81(0)75-541-7025
Mail : yumekoubouantique@gmail.com
URL : www.yumekoobou.com

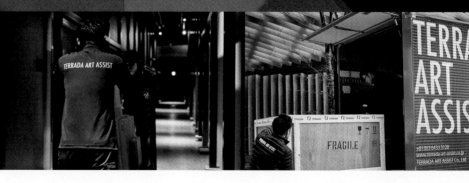

ME NO ME

SINCE 1977

Japanese Arts and Antiques

Publisher
Satoshi Sakurai

Editors
Takehide Ito
Hiroyoshi Ando
Koko Kobayashi
Kazusa Koike

English Edition Coordinator
Masa Kuji (BBL)

Art Director & Designer
Yoshikazu Kasai (DBS Inc.)

Translators
Masa Kuji (BBL)
Katsu Takahashi (BBL)

English Editor
Sam Mitani

Editorial Coordinator
Akiko Ito

Advertising Sales & Promotion
Keisuke Kobayashi
Motomu Ishii

ME NO ME Co., Ltd.

4F Marui Bldg. 2-5-13, Azabujuban,
Minato-ku, Tokyo 106-0045 Japan

Tel. 81-(0) 3-6721-1152
Fax. 81-(0)3-6721-1153

info@menomeonline.com

Follow us

@menome1977

@menome1977

@menomeonline

SUBSCRIBE

ME NO ME (Japanese edition) available for purchase.
ME NO ME (Japanese edition) is a monthly publication (12 issues annually) available for subscription.
Back issues can also be purchased subject to availability.

Subscription package

- 1 year subscription
- Japan : JPY 10,000 (tax and shipping included)
- Outside of Japan : JPY 10,000 (tax included) + shipping (shipping cost varies by region)

* Subscription cannot be cancelled during subscription term

Back issue

Back issues can be purchased from the April 2013 issue and onwards. All back issues are subject to availability. Please inquire for availability.

How to order

Please visit our website

https://menomeonline.com

or contact us by
Email to : info@menomeonline.com
Tel. 81-(0)3-6721-1152
Fax. 81-(0)3-6721-1153

Printing: Shoei Printing Co., Ltd.